LIFE'S LESSONS
FROM A CANDY MACHINE

Darrell Maloney

Copyright 2012 by Darrell Maloney

The Candy Machine

It really wasn't anything special to look at, as far as candy machines went. An older model from the early 1950s, with a dozen or so pull knobs in front. Each knob was directly below a particular candy bar or flavor of chewing gum, which was encased behind a curved clear plastic window.

Above the displayed samples of goodies was the single word "Candy," written in large brown script, beginning in the lower left portion of the machine, then extending upward at an angle, terminating at the upper right corner. The bottom of the letter "y" curved and swept below the other letters.

Today this machine, if it still exists, probably sits in an antique store somewhere, or as a prop in a themed restaurant. Back then, when I was a kid, it belied its nondescript appearance, for it wasn't just any machine, but a magical wonder. For this particular machine often gave up its treasure of snacks for free.

I don't remember when we first discovered the flaw in the machine. But we knew about it and took advantage of it periodically for at least a couple of years. The machine sat nonchalantly inside the Conoco station on 34th Street and Avenue X, which we walked past twice daily on our way to and from elementary school.

Each way on our way home from school, we had a habit of stopping in the Conoco station to drink ice cold water from the fountain, or to watch the mechanic repair a flat tire. We volunteered many times to help the attendant pump gas, but he would never let us. In those days there was no such thing as "self-service." The attendant pumped gas for the customer, and it looked like great fun. These days, as we all know only too well, it isn't.

Anyway, back to the candy machine. We made a point of hanging around the office until both the attendant and the mechanic were busy, then reaching hopefully for the knobs on the machine. Most of the time, the knobs would stop halfway out, that would be the end of it, and we'd be on our way. But occasionally, something would get stuck in the machine, or a locking mechanism would be displaced, or a coin would get jammed inside. We were never sure what caused the occasional malfunction. Whatever it was, it sometimes allowed the knobs to pull completely out, dislodging a candy bar and dropping it into the chute below. Free.

Knowing it was wrong, but never letting our consciences get in the way of free candy bars, we'd take three or four bars each, stuff them into our pockets, and head for home. We'd joyfully eat the candy, never once stopping to think that someone else would eventually have to pay for it.

All of this abruptly stopped when I was about ten. My pal Kent and I had just relieved the machine of five or six candy bars, and turned around to find the not-so-friendly face of Mr. Pollard, the station owner. He had just stepped out from the back room to take a break from inventorying parts, and caught us red-handed and red-faced.

Because we liked Mr. Pollard, and because he had always been kind to us, it hurt even more to see the look of sadness and disappointment that came across his face. He said he thought we knew better than to steal from a friend. It then dawned on us that yes, we had been stealing, and yes, we had been doing it from someone we cared about. Our elation about the free candy turned quickly to disgust with ourselves and our actions. Normally when I got into trouble, my primary concern was the terrible punishment in store for me after I got home. This situation, though, was different. I remember my only worry was that I had lost the friendship of a kind and gentle man who was never too busy to answer the questions of a young boy curious about how to repair an engine, or how the gas pump worked, or how gasoline was made.

Mr. Pollard didn't lose his temper. He calmly reached out his hand for the candy bars we held, and told us to follow him. To the back room we went with him, where he provided us with something we needed much more than candy: the chance to earn back his trust. We spent the next two hours counting air filters and PCV valves and spark plugs, while he logged the numbers on his inventory sheet.

For several weeks after that, Kent and I reported promptly to Mr. Pollard after school. He would hand each of us a bright red mechanic's rag to use when checking the oil in his customers' cars. We'd wash the customers' windows, and we'd sweep and mop the office floor. We'd straighten the free maps in the map dispenser and answer the telephone when it rang.

One day Mr. Pollard thanked us for our work and told us that he'd hoped we learned a lesson. Indeed we had. It was a lesson I remember vividly still today.

I lost track of Mr. Pollard when he retired a few years later, but I still remember him well. I can close my eyes and picture his tall, sturdy frame as clearly as that day I turned around to find him standing behind me. I still have great respect for the man for the dignified way of handling a difficult situation, and for helping keep two young boys on the straight and narrow.

The Shuffler

I vividly remember how cool and inviting the dirty green water looked on that hot summer afternoon. Although most of what happened during the rest of that day remains a blur even now, the memory of that still water beckoning me toward it still lives in my mind as though it happened this morning.

The four of us: myself and my friends Dennis, Jimmy and Wesley, were on the south end of Clapp Lake, standing at the end of a storm runoff, watching what was left of the previous day's rainstorm trickle into the lake. We'd started out on the opposite end of the water that morning, fishing at our favorite spot, but the fish weren't biting. I suppose the heavy rains the day before had them all riled up, as the rain tended to do, or perhaps they just didn't want to bite that day. As the afternoon sun climbed higher in the sky, and the humidity became more and more unbearable, we finally gave up on fishing, stashed our gear behind some shrubs, and went for a walk around the lake.

There was a swimming pool at the southeast corner of Clapp Park, but we had no money that day. And so it was that instead of fishing, instead of going to the pool, we found ourselves standing at the end of that long concrete runoff, peering into that dirty green water as she beckoned us to join her.

We'd never been swimming in this lake before. We didn't know any of her features, or how deep the water was. But one of us had to go first. Wesley dared me to do it, and in those days I rarely passed up a dare. The last two things I still remember clearly of that day were removing my shoes and socks, and taking off my shirt. Then diving head first into that cold green water.

The rest, as I said, is a blur even today. I hit something on the bottom of the lake, squarely on the top of my head, and I hit it very hard. I vaguely remember thinking "damn, it's not deep enough," and the sensation of losing control of my body. I quite literally saw stars, just like on the cartoons, only this wasn't funny. I felt the sensation of water being sucked into my lungs, and of everything going black, and struggling to get my head out of the water. Only my body wasn't cooperating. I couldn't seem to move my arms at all, and my legs had become lead weights.

Next was the feeling of severe nausea. I was somehow on the grass next to the lake, finally out of the water. And I was laying on my side and throwing up, heaving wave after wave of that sweet green water. I kept heaving long after the water had left my lungs, as though my body wanted to make sure it expelled every last drop. I was dizzy and dazed, my head was pounding mightily, and the top of my skull felt like it was on fire.

I very groggily looked around, still unsure of who I was or what had just happened, and I saw the shocked faces of my friends, and the improbable tears in Wesley's eyes. For some inexplicable reason that I still don't understand, I turned my head away from my friends, and saw the back of an old man shuffling slowly away in a gray striped suit. Over his shoulder he instructed my friends, "get him home to his mother, boys, so she can take a look at that head."

My head. It was still pounding, and still on fire. I reached my hand to the top of my head, and it came back covered in blood. I was suddenly very cold despite the oppressive heat, and began to shiver almost uncontrollably.

I was helped to my feet and stumbled home with the aid of my friends, barefoot for the entire twelve blocks. Someone carried my shoes and socks and shirt, although I can't remember exactly who. I know I didn't carry them, and yet they were there beside me when my mother washed the top of my head half an hour later.

Little had been said on that long walk home. We all realized what had almost happened, so no words were necessary. I was incapable of conversation anyway, and I occupied my thoughts not with my friends, but with the old man shuffling away in that gray striped suit. Even in my semi-conscious state, he'd looked so familiar. I'd seen that shuffle before.

I lost my grandfather when I was four years old, and have very few recollections of him. I vaguely remember his laugh, and the way he'd let me rub his shiny bald head. How he'd go through his pockets and give me nickels. He was a deacon at the Colgate Street Church of Christ where we attended service each Sunday morning, and I have vague memories of him getting up from the pews at a certain point during each service. He'd meet other members of the congregation at the back of the church, and they would each take a stack of collection plates. I recall watching him each Sunday, shuffling up the aisle of the church, passing the plates to each row of people to collect their offerings. Shuffling in that old gray striped suit of his.

It was the only suit I ever saw him wear, and I found out later that it was the only suit he had. And the one they buried him in.

In the days following the incident at the lake, my friends helped me to understand what had happened that day. I had hit my head on a rock at the bottom of the lake, and after what seemed like eternity to them, I resurfaced, thrashing wildly in the water, unaware of my surroundings, and unable to get to shore. Dennis and Wesley finally were able to drag me from the water, but I was unconscious by then. They laid me on the grass and Jimmy ran off to find help.

Dennis said they turned around and found the old man in the gray striped suit walking up behind them. They said he seemed to come out of nowhere, and said very little. But he seemed to know exactly what to do. He gently brushed my friends aside and rolled me onto my stomach, then repeatedly pressed both sides of my abdomen with such force that Wesley thought he'd break my back.

Dennis said that after a couple of minutes, I started to cough. Weakly at first, he said. Then violently. Then I started to throw up the lake water. He said it seemed like gallons.

He didn't have to tell me the rest. The rest I knew, as vague as it was. That awful feeling of pain and nausea. Watching that old man shuffling slowly away in a familiar gray striped suit.

I went back to Clapp Lake several times over the course of that summer and fall of 1968. I don't know what I was looking for, exactly. My friends went with me a couple of times. Other times I went alone, because they told me that part of the lake gave them the willies after what had happened.

I guess what I wanted more than anything was to find that old man, who appeared out of nowhere, just in time to save my life and disappear again. I wanted to find out who he was, where he came from, where he went. I wanted to find out if... well, I guess it's not important.

I developed a fear of water that summer. For a long time I wouldn't go in a pool, and when I did it took me a while to get up the courage to put my head below the water. I eventually got over it. But I never forgot that incident at Clapp Lake, nor that old man and the way he shuffled away with that old familiar shuffle. And to this day, every time I'm in Lubbock I drive by that spot on the south end of the lake and wonder...

A Most Amazing Coincidence

I was thumbing through my second wife's seventh grade yearbook not long ago when I was still married and living in Atlanta. It was a lazy afternoon, and we were between my two favorite seasons. That is to say, football was already over and baseball hadn't yet begun.

A strikingly beautiful woman, Jane's eyes held a certain spark that highlighted her face, and her smile could warm even the coldest heart. I wanted to see if she'd always looked that way.

When I picked up Jane's old yearbook, it immediately separated from its once-bound cover. Ripped and dog-eared, it had obviously seen better days. I carefully put it back together and gazed at the cover of this piece of my wife's own personal history.

"Warrior Pride, 1972," the cover announced. The school mascot was a native American chief, profiled in red in a splendid feathered headdress. The overleaf announced that the book came from Fernwood Junior High School in Biloxi, Mississippi. I'd never been to Biloxi myself, and had only driven through Mississippi on my way to and from other places. Still, I had known others who had lived in Mississippi, so it's surprising that I made no mental connection at that time.

On this particular Sunday afternoon, I was drawn by curiosity. I'd never seen a photograph of Jane in her adolescent years. I'd seen photos of her in high school, and knew that she'd been a knockout. I'd seen baby pictures, and noted that even as a toddler her smile was one to spread sunshine on the darkest day. But all those years in between were missing. What was she like in junior high school?

So here I was, looking through the pages, trying to find my sweetheart as she looked in 1972. I easily found the seventh grade section of the book, and flipped page by page to the Ws, where I knew I would find a young Jane Waugh.

Sure enough, her warm smile beamed up at me from the page below, and I thought, were I at that particular school at that particular time, I'd have wanted this sweet young beauty to be my girlfriend.

Then I started leafing through the pages, as one tends to do with old yearbooks, to laugh at old hairdos and to try to find other photographs of my wife engaged in school activities.

As I scanned across a page full of heads and shoulders a couple of pages back from Jane's class photo, my eyes stopped short and stuck on a particular face, and a chill ran up my spine. This was another face I'd seen before. Many, many times.

Dumbstruck and disbelieving, I looked at the name below the photo, although I knew deep down inside there could be no mistake. The name: Barbara Ratliff. My first wife.

I met Barbara in my sophomore year of high school, in Lubbock, Texas. We dated throughout high school, and married six months after graduation, in late 1977.

My marriage to Barbara lasted six years, and produced two wonderful children, before we finally decided that the marriage had been a mistake. We were much too young when we married, and weren't as compatible as we'd thought. For the betterment of all concerned, we went our separate ways. Over the years, however, we remained good friends.

It was a full year after my divorce from Barbara was final, when I was living in Victorville, California, that Jane first caught my eye. It was an office romance which blossomed into a deep, undying love. She'd been going through her own divorce at that time, and we developed our relationship slowly at first, afraid of rushing into another commitment that perhaps wasn't meant to be.

But the wonders of fate knew what they were doing. By the time we'd visited Cairo, Egypt, some months later in the summer of 1985, we were close enough to express our love for each other. On our way back from Egypt, on a little island in the Azores, we found ourselves giggling like little school children, playing on a swing set in a darkened playground at 3 a.m., oblivious to the world and those who would say this wasn't normal behavior. It was at that moment that I decided I wanted to spend the rest of my life with this woman.

Jane and I were married in 1986 and began our extended honeymoon together. It was many years later that I decided to pick up that yearbook and discovered that she and Barbara had been classmates in Biloxi, Mississippi, in 1972. Until that day I had no clue.

Neither, for that matter, did they. When I pointed out what I consider to be the most amazing of coincidences, they both reacted in the same way. First, they didn't believe me. There must be some mistake, they said. Yes, they did attend that particular school at that particular time in their lives, but it was not possible for (insert name here) to have been there also. After all, neither remembered the other.

Faced with the evidence, the book itself, their disbelief turned to amazement. Given the odds of such a thing happening, they were both incredulous. As for me, having chosen as my wives two women I'd met in different parts of the country, nine years apart, who'd sat in the same classroom together when they were 13 years old, was just mind-boggling to me. But it happened.

Not long after my discovery, Jane was going to throw out the yearbook. "It's falling apart," she said, "and I no longer have a use for it."

I should have kept my mouth shut, but I still haven't learned to do that. I made the mistake of telling my dear, sweet, wonderful wife that I wanted her to keep the book. "After all," I joked, "I might want to look through it someday to see what my next wife looked like in 1972. She's bound to be in there somewhere."

Turns out she had a use for the book after all. She hit me over the head with it.

War Heroes and Football Games

The Vietnam War years were, to be sure, a turbulent time in American history. But for a kid growing up in that era, as I did, it had little significance, because I wasn't directly affected by it.

I saw the protests on the nightly news, courtesy of Walter Cronkite, Chet Huntley and David Brinkley. I knew that young men were picketing the White House, burning their draft cards, or running off to other countries to avoid military duty. But since I didn't have any older brothers to get caught up in the draft, the problem that was Vietnam seemed a world away.

My hometown of Lubbock, Texas, was considered a military town in that an Air Force pilot training base was located just outside the city limits. Despite that, I can't recall seeing many Air Force people in town during my childhood. I'm sure they were there, as many of them undoubtedly lived in the city. But they didn't often wear their uniforms in public. Had I been older, this might have struck me as odd. But since I was merely a kid, it never really registered.

I think the lack of a visible military presence in my neighborhood helps explain why I was so impressed the first time I met a real, honest to goodness, Vietnam veteran.

Larry and I used to hang out together a lot in the last years of grade school. I helped him throw newspapers along his neighborhood route, and we blew up model airplanes with firecrackers, played chess and Stratego, and a hundred other things that boys do to occupy their time.

Larry and I also shared a love for sports, particularly football, and played quite often with Dennis and Jimmy and the other boys in the neighborhood.

One day Larry suggested we walk over to another of his friends' house to play ball.

Matthew Roberts lived several blocks away, in what we considered at the time to be a "rich" neighborhood. The houses on Matthew's street were easily three times larger than ours, and were made of brick or stone, where ours were covered with slate shingles, coated with thirty years or more of periodic paint jobs.

In a boy's mind, such differences constitute social and economic boundaries, and we tended to erect invisible walls between ourselves and the kids who lived in such neighborhoods. I suppose this was partly because we didn't want to be reminded of the things we wanted but could not have. In any event, we never made a great effort to make friends with the "rich kids," even though they lived only a few streets away from us.

Another thing Matthew's house had was a rather large front yard, perfect for playing football.

We were well into our game that day, and enjoying it thoroughly, when Matthew's father stepped out of a car and walked up the driveway. In a magnificent display of military bearing, he wore his Army dress green uniform with obvious pride. Every medal was perfectly aligned, each crease was sharp and straight, and his brass buttons shone brightly in the late afternoon sun.

It was impossible not to have respect for this man, our one and only example of a Vietnam veteran. He had just returned from the war, and was on leave spending time with his family before going back for a second tour.

The look in Mr. Robert's eyes reflected a hardened man, who had seen things young boys didn't need to know about. Yet his eyes were deceiving, for his demeanor was that of a kind and gentle man, who patiently answered our questions about Army life, what he did to earn all the stripes on his arm, and what it was like to travel all over the world.

Matthew's dad played football in the front yard with us, still decked out in his full dress uniform. After awhile he went into the house, and I never saw him again.

I remember thinking how lucky Matthew was to have this dignified war hero for a father, and I learned a couple of things, although I almost certainly didn't realize it at the time.

One is that fathers in general are heroes in little boys' eyes, whether they go off to fight an unpopular war, or stay at home to grind out a living for their families. My own father certainly fell into this category, and over time I learned to appreciate how physically demanding his job as a letter carrier for the postal service was. I'm reminded of that more and more today, as I visit with him and notice that this man who once stood as tall and sturdy as a fifty-year oak is now slightly stooped and in pain from twenty-odd years of carrying an 80-pound leather bag for six hours a day.

The other thing I learned is that it isn't a house that makes a person rich, but the family ties that exist within that house. Matthew Roberts was indeed fortunate, but it wasn't because he lived in a house that was three times the size of my own. It was because he had parents who were close, and who cared for him, as he did for them.

Matthew and I grew apart as we got older, as did Larry and I. Matthew became a talented athlete, and was a captain on the Lubbock High School football team the year before I graduated. No doubt the product of a lot of days playing ball with his father, the war hero.

It's funny that as we grow older we realize how childhood friendships and experiences shape the way we feel about things today. It's also funny how a walk down memory lane can bring about a strong desire to look up old friends and relive old memories.

Larry Lindstrom and Matthew Roberts, I know you're out there somewhere. If you read this, please get word to me. I'd like to shake your hand again, and buy you a drink.

And talk about war heroes...

The Great Gasoline Caper

Some of the fondest memories of my youth were the pranks my friends and I would play on the people in my old neighborhood. No one was immune to these practical jokes, and while some of them may appear stupid in retrospect, they were all intended as good clean fun.

As I said, no one was immune, and we were just as likely to fall victim to our friends' jokes as anyone else.

So were our parents.

Some of the pranks worked better than others. We once played a prank on Kent Dobkins' father that became a classic, and was still the subject of conversation well into our high school years.

We used to earn extra spending money by mowing peoples' lawns during the warm weather months. More often than not, when we'd run low on gas for our lawnmower, we'd siphon the fuel we needed from my father's car, or from Wesley's dad's pickup truck.

We used a length of water line about a quarter inch in diameter that Dad had left over when he'd installed the swamp cooler on our house. It was the perfect size to siphon fuel, since it was small enough to roll up and stick in the back pocket of our jeans, but filled a three-gallon gas can in about ten minutes flat.

By the way, I should provide a warning to the kids: don't try this at home. Gas is extremely poisonous (I found out later), and siphoning it as we did back then occasionally meant we accidentally got a mouthful of the stuff. More than once we wound up swallowing some, and paid the price with nausea and a bad headache for a couple of days. Also, back then gas contained lead, and I'm convinced that the frequent lapses of memory I suffer today are a result of the gasoline I swallowed when I was a boy.

Kent had seen Wesley and I steal gas from our fathers on several occasions, and one afternoon he made an innocent comment which spawned what would become one of our finest pranks.

"If y'all have any left over, why don't you put it in my dad's car? He's always complaining that it drinks more gas than it should."

Almost immediately, Wesley got a look of pure evil on his face. It was obvious that he'd hatched a plan.

Wesley's scheme was simple. We'd siphon out two or three gallons from our fathers' fuel tanks every couple or three days and add the gas to Kent's father's car at night when he was watching television. After awhile, he'd notice that his car wasn't burning any gas, and he'd think he was getting great gas mileage.

The joke worked perfectly. After about the fourth night, the Dobkins' fuel tank was full, and it was just a matter of topping it off every couple of days to keep it that way.

After a week or so, Kent reported that his father thanked his mother at the dinner table for putting gas in the family car for him. When she denied doing so, he scratched his head, went outside to look at the car, and came back to announce that the fuel gauge must be broken.

Kent was with his father the next day when he went to Mr. Pollard's Conoco station to fill up what he thought had to be a nearly-empty tank.

Back then, gas pumps didn't have automatic cutoffs, and the service station attendant didn't get more than a gallon into the tank before gas gushed out to soak his trousers. He was a bit upset with Mr. Dobkins, who adamantly argued that the tank must be about dry.

Mr. Dobkins, on the other hand, couldn't believe his luck. After driving for more than two weeks, he'd only used a gallon of gas. This was phenomenal gas mileage.

Kent's dad bragged to everyone he knew about his car and the mileage he got. Kent came over one day to tell us that his Uncle Ted didn't believe Kent's father, and that his father challenged his brother to take the car, drive it for a couple of weeks, and see for himself.

We thought the jig was up, until two weeks later when Uncle Ted brought the car back, told Kent's father he was insane and owed him five dollars for gas, and an argument ensued between the two.

From that point on, we started taking gas out of the car.

Kent's father, upset that his once-economical automobile was now drinking gasoline like nobody's business, blamed his brother for his sudden drop in gas mileage. Kent reported that his father told Uncle Ted he was no longer welcome in their house. That was fine with Kent, since he didn't much like his uncle anyway.

Kent never told his father about the prank, and when they moved out of the neighborhood several years later, it was still our secret.

If I ever stumble across Kent again, I don't think I'll reintroduce myself, shake his hand, and relive old times. Instead, I think I'll sneak into his driveway every few nights and pour gas into his fuel tank.

I want to see how long it'll take for him to catch on.

Easter at Casa Maloney

Easter was always a special time of the year at my house, not because of the religious connotations, but because it was one of the few times each year when our parents bought us candy. It was also one of the few times when all of my siblings, and our cousins who lived in Lubbock, met and did something together. The only other time this happened in my childhood was at Christmas.

The location of our Easter egg hunt varied from year to year, but the procedure was always the same. My father, and whichever of my uncles came along that year, would select a local park, and everyone would meet there at a specified time. Then the men would get out of their cars to hide the eggs, the women would gather outside to socialize, and the kids would remain inside the cars.

We were always counseled not to peek, and dutifully placed our hands over our eyes. My sisters and the other girls always kept their faces tightly covered and their eyes closed. My brother Randy and I, and the rest of the boys, would peek through our fingers. We'd watch very closely where most of the eggs were going, and in particular we all watched our Uncle Bob like a hawk.

We'd learned from previous hunts that Uncle Bob tired quickly of this chore each year. While his brothers took great care to find good hiding places for their baskets of candy and eggs, Bob would toss a few here and there, hide a couple in the weeds, and then dump most of the basket near a tree or under a piece of playground equipment. To see where Uncle Bob did his annual candy dump greatly increased the chance of striking the candy mother lode.

Being fast was the other prerequisite, of course. I ran much faster than Randy, and faster than all of my cousins except for Jerry. Each year it was a mad dash between Jerry and I to see who got to Uncle Bob's dump site the fastest. The first one there, of course, got the upper hand in gathering up the pile of goodies. Whichever of us got there second still had good pickings, but didn't get quite so much. My siblings and other cousins would scramble around the park, each trying to gather as many of the other eggs and candy they could find.

Most of our eggs were the colored, marshmallow variety, individually wrapped in cellophane. There were also a couple of dozen boiled eggs, brightly colored, that my Aunt Nell would bring.

We, of course, preferred the candy eggs. We'd pick up the boiled eggs only if we happened to be bending over for a candy egg at the same spot and it was convenient, or after all the candy eggs had already been claimed.

It wasn't that we didn't like the boiled eggs; it's just that, given a choice between food and candy, a kid will almost always choose candy.

My father had a habit of selecting a few marshmallow eggs and embedding them with nickels and dimes. He'd usually throw in a quarter or two as a grand prize. He'd take the coins and force them through the wrapper and into the egg. Not very hygienic, but hey, we were kids. We didn't care. We did have to be sure to inspect the eggs closely before we bit into them, though. The dimes were small enough to disappear completely into the egg, remaining hidden until it was time to chip one of our teeth.

This tradition, slightly modified, was passed on to my children when they hunted eggs years later. By that time, we had the hard plastic eggs that separated in the middle. We always bought several dozen of these, filled them with jelly beans or other candy, and placed our spare change into a selected few.

My children, not surprisingly, did the same thing with the boiled eggs that Randy and I used to do: open them up, eat the yoke, and deposit the rest into the nearest garbage can.

For my own childrens' egg hunts, the hard plastic eggs weren't the only high-tech innovation we incorporated. We let them use actual, honest to goodness, Easter baskets. My siblings and cousins and I always used medium sized paper grocery bags, rolled down two or three times at the opening to make them easier to hold onto. Prepared this way, they looked like an upside-down version of our pant-legs, which were rolled *up* two or three times so we could wear them longer (or, as my dad used to say, "grow into them").

Of course, we had seen other kids at the parks with Easter baskets back in the early 1960s. I therefore know that such baskets existed, and my sisters each wanted one very badly. I didn't care one way or the other. As long as I had a place to deposit my spoils, I was happy. I didn't much care what it looked like.

Every year when the weather started to turn nice and Easter Sunday approached, my sisters would ask my mom and dad if they would buy them real Easter baskets that year. My parents always did the same thing. They would look at each other, and say "Easter baskets?" without the hint of a smile, and pretend they didn't have any earthly idea what the girls were referring to. They'd ask one of my sisters to describe the baskets in detail, and then they'd say they'd watch out for them at the grocery store. Of course, they never found any, and Easter Sunday would again have my sisters using the same kind of paper grocery bags that Randy and I had.

The first couple of times they did this, I thought they were just playing a prank on my sisters. Over the years, though, I've decided that it was just their way of staying within our very tight budget by not promising or buying frivolous things. After all, the baskets I bought my own kids were only used once and then thrown in the garbage can. That just wasn't the way my cost-conscious parents did things.

Like Christmas and Halloween, we ended up with a fair-sized pile of goodies when the day was done. Our folks didn't believe in rationing out candy a little at a time. I found out later that they secretly hoped we'd gorge ourselves to the point of nausea, swear off candy forever, and stop asking them for it. Not a chance. We ate it as quickly as we could, built up a cast-iron lining within our stomachs, and increased our tolerance for candy. Then we started asking for more of it.

Later, when my children brought home a trick or treat bag or Easter basket full of goodies, my wife and I were always careful to limit the kids' intake to a couple of pieces of candy per day. We did indeed learn something from the mistakes of our parents.

Clapp Park

K.N. Clapp Park rests more or less in the center of my hometown of Lubbock, Texas. Built decades ago on over 250 acres of prime real estate, this park offers something for everyone who enjoys being outdoors.

Little league ball fields, playground equipment, and long stretches of thick, green grass and majestic trees surround two large playa lakes. On the northwest corner of the park, a garden center offers year-round displays of plants and flowers, and a 140 year-old chapel that is still used for weddings and social functions.

On the southeast corner, a public swimming pool gives the city's youth a cool place to play on hot summer days.

Clapp Park holds a special place in my heart, for this is the place where I whiled away many days of my childhood.

The lakes were man-made when my father was a young boy. They are continually refilled by storm water runoff, which washes in from surrounding streets every time it rains. For blocks around the park, streets slope very gently, almost imperceptibly, so that gravity sends the water rolling toward Clapp Park and its twin lakes.

For most of the year, these lakes were merely a relaxing place to fish for perch. Old men and adolescent boys would spend hours sitting on the shoreline, watching little red and white floats bobbing up and down on the gentle wind-blown waves. More often than not, the day would end with nothing being caught, but that was okay. After all, like a wise man once said, a bad day fishing is better than a good day doing anything else.

We had just as much watching the clouds roll by and discussing the meaning of life as we did catching an occasional fish. It was a boy's idea of heaven. If there was a free pizza stand I'd have never left.

On windy days we'd take the small boats we'd carved for the cub scout regatta and race them across the lake. We'd go to the downwind side of the lake, place our boats into the water at the same time, and watch the wind take off with them as we raced around the lake to catch them on the other side. The first boat to touch land on the other side won the race. Since we seldom had money to bet, the losers would fess up something of value. A bag of marbles, a favorite baseball card, a couple of hot wheels cars. We never knew what we were going to get when we won a race, but that's what made it more fun.

My friend Wesley, who we'd nicknamed "the Brain" several years before, once decided to race his boat without its sail. He had read a book about aerodynamics, and decided that his boat would be so sleek and smooth without the sail to encumber it, that it would fly across the lake in half the time. We all looked at each other, but none of us said anything. It was like being handed a free piece of cake.

Of course all of our boats were picked up and dried off on the other side of the lake before Wesley's was even halfway across. As I remember, we finally went home when it started getting dark, and Wesley's boat was still bobbing slowly up and down fifty yards from shore. He had to go back and get it the next day.

I can't remember why we started calling Wesley "the Brain." From what I saw many times over the years, I suspect it was an early attempt at sarcasm.

Each summer, the city was hit hard with afternoon thunderstorms, sometimes two or three a week. These "gully-washers," as my grandfather would call them, would send torrents of water rushing down the streets, stalling out cars and creating chaos for commuters on their way home from work.

After a handful of these rainstorms, both lakes at Clapp Park would become so swollen that the waters would flood some of the nearby streets for days at a time.

This tended to ruin the fishing, but it gave us many new opportunities to play.

For example, when the playground was under two feet of water, it became quite literally a water park. We'd ride the tall slide down to the lake at its bottom, while our buddies poured buckets of water behind us to keep our wet clothes from sticking. We'd swing from the monkey bars high into the air, then let go and "splash down" like a Gemini space capsule returning to earth.

One day we laughed like crazy when Mark climbed to the top of the slide, stood on the platform, and then began doing what can best be described as a weird mating dance. Then a four-inch fish became dislodged from his shorts and went tumbling down the slide.

When the rainwater washed into the park from the surrounding streets, it was funneled into great concrete causeways, which led to the lake's edge, and gave the water an expedient path to its final destination.

If the rains were heavy enough, these causeways were like river rapids. We'd jump in and let them carry us for fifty yards, then climb back out and race uphill and do it again. More than once I had to explain to my parents how I lost a shoe, since they tended to get sucked right off your feet.

Conversely, sometimes the rains never came, or they were lighter than a typical year. These years, Lubbock would suffer drought-like conditions that would come close to drying up both lakes completely. These were the times when we would explore the dried and cracked mud that normally would have been several feet under water. We'd find fishing hooks and sinkers by the dozen, and I once even found a shoe that I'd lost the previous year.

It was when the lakes were at their lowest that we caught crawdads and had crawdad races. These creatures were gray or brown in color, looked like little lobsters, and made great entertainment for bored adolescent boys.

We'd draw a big circle in chalk on the playground parking lot, and each of us would go down to the lake's edge to find a crawdad. Then we'd put them all in the center of the circle and yell, stomp, and do anything else we could to encourage our charges to run away. The boy whose crawdad crawled out of the chalk circle first was the winner.

At least the crawdads didn't die. We always took them back to the water when we finished with them. The fish in the lake, on the other hand, usually weren't so lucky. When the lakes began to dry up, eventually they would get to the point where there was not enough oxygen to keep the fish alive. Fish started dying and floating on top of the water, and as the water receded the fish would deposit themselves in the drying mud.

Each time this happened, I remember looking at the hundreds of dead and dying fish and wondering where they were the previous spring when we were trying to entice them to nibble on our fishhooks.

Each time the lake would dry up, the parks department would have to restock the lakes the following fall, and the next year's fishing would be even more sparse than normal.

Whenever I visit Lubbock, I always include Clapp Park on my itinerary. Sometimes I'll walk around the lakes, or along the dirt levee that divides them. Other times I'll visit the spot where I almost drowned so many years ago, after diving into the murky water and hitting my head on a rock. Or the west side of the lake where we once dared Wesley to ride his bike off of the concrete pier. It became entangled in some debris on the bottom of the lake, and we had to wait until the next drought to retrieve it. By that time it was so rusty it was worthless, but we replaced all the parts and rebuilt it anyway over the course of several months.

And sometimes I'll just sit in the grass under one of the many trees and watch the ghosts of my friends and I, walking and talking and laughing… making stones skip across the top of the water and arguing about girls and baseball players and a myriad of other things.

Regardless of what else I see when I visit Clapp Park, I am always marveled how little everything has changed over the years. The dirt levee is overgrown with trees now, but its banks are still covered with kids' fishing hooks and floats. The trees are much bigger now, but they're still in the same spots I remember. I haven't tried climbing any of them lately because I know it'll serve to remind me that I've grown as old as they are.

The little league field where I hit my first home run, and struck out for the first time, is gone now, replaced by a monument to the man who organized the first little league in

Lubbock. On the other side of the park is a larger, newer ballpark where kids of today make their own memories.

Someday I hope to be visiting in Lubbock during one of the late spring gully-washers. I want to see if the current generation of kids still go bodysurfing down the causeways.

The Twenty

I've talked before about perspectives and how they change as we get older. The bathroom sink in our elementary school, set at a height for youngsters, still seems way too high for a tiny first grader, standing on his tiptoes, struggling to wash his hands. The same sink, twenty years later, seems impossibly low when that first grader is all grown up and using the restroom after attending a PTA meeting with his own young son.

The same thing applies to money. As a boy of ten, I was happy to have a dollar's worth of change in my pocket. This was partly because a dollar bought a lot more back then. It was also because when I was ten, my needs were a lot simpler, and a dollar's worth of change would cover them all quite nicely.

For example, if I had hunger pangs, I could walk into Pollard's Conoco station and buy a bottle of Coca Cola for ten cents and a candy bar for a nickel. Those were the days before candy bars began to "downsize," and one bar was more than enough to satisfy a kid's sweet tooth.

If my bicycle tire had a flat, I could walk up to the Globe Department Store and buy a patch kit for thirty nine cents. And if I didn't feel like doing my homework that particular day, my buddy Wesley would do it for me for a dime. So, you see, I was set.

These days are different. These days we don't feel comfortable walking out of the house with fewer than three credit cards, a checkbook, and a couple of twenties.

Back in 1970, a twenty dollar bill was something we saw only when our parents were handing it over to the clerk at the grocery store, and then only for a moment. Therefore, when Tony and I found a folded up twenty in the parking lot outside the H.E.B. food store, we couldn't even be sure it was real.

Oh, it looked official enough. It appeared to have everything a one dollar bill had, and was the same size and shape. Still, it looked strangely alien to us. We knew who George Washington was, from our fifth grade history classes. We knew that he was famous for chopping down a cherry tree and then getting his butt blistered by his dad because he couldn't bring himself to lie his way out of it. We thought he was a sap. We also knew that Washington was famous for a couple of other things, but couldn't remember what they were.

Since he was on the one dollar bill, maybe he was the guy who invented money. That must be it.

But it wasn't Washington who stared up at us from this twenty. It was some dude named Jackson, and we'd never heard of him.

"Maybe it's counterfeit," I offered. "Let's go into the H.E.B. and see if we can spend it."

"No, stupid. If it's counterfeit they'll arrest us. Besides, somebody who knows our moms might tell." Tony had a couple of valid points.

Instead, we sat on this bill for several days, unsure what to do with it. Then it finally dawned on us that we could take it to the Stop 'n' Go, a convenience store down on the corner. It was run by a little old man named Walt, and we could easily outrun him if the bill was counterfeit and he tried to hold us for the cops.

But we still ran the risk of running into someone who knew our moms and might tell them we were at the store buying twenty dollars worth of candy and Twinkies. That just wouldn't do.

Our solution was to skip school one afternoon and go when the store was unlikely to be busy.

But what if Walt demanded to know where we managed to get a twenty dollar bill?

Ten year old boys can be awfully paranoid.

We decided to buy something other than goodies, as though one of our moms had sent us to the store for her. Then, once the twenty was broken, the smaller bills would be much easier to use without arousing suspicion. It was a brilliant plan.

We cut school the next day and hung around the back of the Stop 'n' Go until only Walt's car was in the parking lot. Then we nonchalantly walked into the store and began browsing for something that looked like an item a mom would send her kid to the store for.

"What kind of mayonnaise did your mom want?" Tony asked in a voice way too loud, since I was standing right next to him. It was for Walt's benefit.

"Miracle Whip." I replied in an equally loud voice. Walt must have thought we were both nearly deaf.

We took the jar of Miracle Whip to the counter and checked out without incident, getting nineteen dollars and some change back, and a "thank you" from Walt.

We were almost to the door when Walt's voice caught up with us. "Hey, wait a minute." We slowly turned.

"Aren't you guys supposed to be in school?"

Tony was good at thinking on his feet. "No sir, they let us out early for a teachers conference."

Walt seemed satisfied with the answer, and we told him goodbye and left the store.

It seemed a waste to throw away the Miracle Whip we'd paid fifty nine cents for, so we ate a good portion of it, right out of the jar, with a couple of spoons we pilfered from the Dairy Queen. It wasn't bad.

Today that Stop 'n' Go is a boarded up and abandoned building, and I'm sure that Walt long ago went to the big convenience store in the sky. But as long as I'm around, they'll both live on, if only in my memories.

Fina With Pflash

Long, long ago, in a land far, far away, there was an advertising campaign that combined a catchy jingle with a cute little slogan, and sent English teachers everywhere searching for their bottles of extra-strength Anacin.

The "long ago" was the late 1960s. The "land far, far away" was actually the United States, but should have been whatever planet those advertising yahoos were on when they launched the campaign. The reason the English teachers were searching for their aspirin was because Fina was trying to undo all the hard work they'd spent teaching America's youth how to spell.

The ad campaign: "Fina with Pflash... Pfantastic!"

Those of you who were around back then will probably remember it. It was everywhere you looked: on billboards, the radio, and all three stations on the television set. Fina even gave out bumper stickers, free of charge, to anyone who wanted them.

When we heard about the free stickers, we decided to walk to the nearest Fina station, which was several blocks away. Kids like things that are free, and things that stick. Something that is free *and* sticks is just something you can't possibly pass up. So we walked up 34th Street, past the First Federal Savings and Loan building, past Dr. Day's chiropractor's office and the dilapidated apartment buildings to the Fina station, where we meekly asked the attendant for a bumper sticker.

"I've got four boxes of them in the corner," he said, pointing with his thumb as he pumped gas into a patron's car. "Take as many as you want."

That was probably the wrong choice of words, but we took him up on his offer, and each of us stuffed the stickers into the back pockets of our jeans. Then we carried away as many as our hands would hold.

Within a couple of days, these stickers were plastered all over fences, garbage cans, and even the windows at our elementary school.

I gave one of the colorful stickers to my friend Wesley, who made the mistake of affixing it to his notebook. Mr. Autry, our principal, saw Wesley's notebook, thought he'd found the culprit who'd plastered the school windows, and made Wesley stay after school that day to help the janitors scrape them off.

Problem was, this was one of the few times when Wesley was completely innocent. He wasn't even with us when we stickered the school. We, of course, thought this was hilarious. Wesley didn't.

Due process isn't normally a part of the typical elementary school justice system. Wesley was so upset by the ordeal that he spent the next couple of weeks plotting various types of revenge against Mr. Autry.

The revenge he finally decided on was to catch a fish at Clapp Lake, let it get just rotten enough to smell really bad, and sneak it into the principal's car on a very hot day, where he'd hide it under the seat.

Fortunately for Mr. Autry, it rained heavily the day Wesley skipped school to go fishing, the fish weren't biting, and he never got a nibble.

After the fiendishly foolish foul fish foil failed, (say that three times...) Wesley calmed down, and never exacted his revenge.

Anyway, back on track...

The "Pflash" campaign was a catchy jingle, but tended to get a bit annoying when you heard it twenty times a day. I don't know if it increased sales for Fina Oil Company, but it sure did increase their name recognition.

Around this same time, my fourth grade teacher gave us a spelling test which included the word "fantastic." Obviously annoyed by Fina's butchering of the word, she warned us ahead of time: "Anyone who puts a 'p' at the beginning of this word will automatically fail the test." Then she went back to her desk and popped a couple of aspirin.

I saw one of those original Fina Pflash stickers on a table at a swap meet a couple of years ago. The vendor, who was a well-known local seller of old movie posters, magazines, and other memorabilia, wanted five dollars for this item. I wasn't willing to pay that much for it, but there's no doubt in my feeble little mind that someone else did. It made me wish we had taken all those bumper stickers and put them away in a box instead of decorating the city of Lubbock.

The ad campaign was resurrected to a limited degree in the mid-1970s. I was reminded of this the last time I looked through the 1975 edition of The Westerner, my high school yearbook. Toward the back of the book is a photograph of the school, with a Fina station in the background. A large sign at the station proclaimed "Fina: Pfantastic!"

Another sign at the same station said the gas was 48 cents a gallon. That's something we'll never see again. I think the same goes for "Pfina with Pflash." At least I hope so...

Electric Football

A typical twelve-year old boy today is immersed in an electronic culture which stops just short of ruling his life. Tell him he's played enough Wii or Super Nintendo, and he'll simply migrate to the television set, where he'll casually surf through 150 channels of worthless programming. Then he'll settle on... a cartoon about the Mario Brothers.

This didn't happen overnight. We've eased into it over the last 30 years or so. The first step in our long journey into social demise was the invention of the remote control.

The first remote control was attached to the television with a long black cable. They made it black on purpose so you couldn't see it at night and would trip over it. It was advertised as being the ultimate in convenience, since you no longer had to get up from the couch to change the channel on your television set.

What the sinister conspirators in the television manufacturing and broadcasting worlds didn't mention was that this was merely the first step in a long-term plan to control our minds. They wanted to turn us into zombies whose sole purpose in life was to lay on the couch, eat potato chips, and gain weight while yelling at our children to move their heads because they were blocking the screen.

The television and remote control led to cable, which began to feed viewers' insatiable appetites for the arcane. This, of course, led to the VCR, and the bane of all mankind, the Beta format.

Beta almost killed the recorded movie industry, in the same way the 8-track tape almost killed recorded music. These two country cousins, Beta and 8-track, were the black sheep of their respective industrial families. Were it not for those mistakes, we'd have progressed much faster into the mindless drones that we are today.

The VCR provided the final incentive for couch potatoes everywhere to spend every waking hour in the reclined position. Now cinematic classics like "Saturday Night Fever" and "I was a Teenaged Werewolf" could be watched according to our own schedule, and as many times in a row as we desired.

Of course this led to our becoming spoiled for entertainment that fit our respective schedules and endless desire for the tasteless and the monotonous. To feed this ever-growing monster, some bright young inventor introduced a game called Pong, the video game revolution was born, and every child's mind automatically turned irrevocably into vanilla pudding.

Okay, I'm far off my intended subject. This was supposed to be about the electronic game of my generation, the holy grail of a 1960s boy's life, the electric football game.

You know the one I'm talking about. You've seen them at your neighborhood garage sales, missing half the pieces, or being hawked at antique shows. Today they are relics, but when I was twelve, they were the ultimate in entertainment, and one of the few things capable of dragging us away from the playground.

Technologically speaking, there wasn't much to this marvel of the '60s. It was about two feet long by eighteen inches or so wide, and consisted of only four components: a sheet metal playing field, painted green with yard lines; a small electric motor mounted under the field which caused the field to vibrate; a plastic frame built around the field, preventing little boys from cutting themselves on the sharp metal edges; and a handful of plastic players.

The players, as the name implies, were molded pieces of plastic made to resemble, well... football players. They were cast in classic NFL poses of the era. Running backs had a ball tucked under one arm and the other arm outstretched, ready to "stiff-arm" a potential tackler. Linemen had both fists clenched and pressed against their sternum, elbows up, to block the opposing team's players. Quarterbacks posed with their passing arm outstretched, as though ready to release a "bomb" the length of the field at any second.

These players could be painted in your own team's colors. Mine, of course, were in Dallas Cowboy blue and silver.

They could also be numbered to resemble miniature versions of your gridiron heroes. Number 17, Dandy Don Meredith, shared the quarterback position on my field with Craig Morton. "Bullet Bob" Hayes caught the touchdown passes, and Walt Garrison racked up the rushing yards.

At each player's feet was a small plastic base, which held half a dozen appendages on the bottom. For whatever reason, we called these things "feelers," and I suppose that name was as good as any other. These feelers could be adjusted in a variety of ways, and each adjustment determined how the player moved when the field began to vibrate. Turn one feeler slightly to the left, and the player would turn sharply to the right. Bend another and he'd run a long hook pattern. We spent many an afternoon planning strategies and adjusting the feelers, in an endless attempt to create the perfect electric football team.

The goal, of course, was to have your blockers push opposing players out of the way so your ball carrier could make it to the end zone untouched. Any contact with the defense meant he was tackled and the play would be whistled dead.

It made for an interesting way to spend an afternoon.

In my father's generation, boys walked to one anothers' houses carrying bags of marbles. With these, they would spend lazy summer days shooting their favorite "cat's eye" in an effort to win their friends' marbles, and go home with their own marble bag a bit heavier. Our variation on this theme was to bet our best players on the game. The winner always had his pick of the loser's players, which he could take home, repaint in his own team's colors, and use against the loser the next time they played. My Craig Morton changed hands so many times he eventually stopped moving at all. Eight coats of paint will do that to you.

Looking back, as much fun as this electronic marvel was, it still didn't compare with going to a vacant lot with a ragged football and actually playing the game ourselves. I guess that's why I worry so much about kids these days. In my day, indoor electronic games were an occasional treat that only temporarily kept us away from exercising our young bodies on the athletic fields. Today, it's the other way around.

Carlsbad Caverns

I guess the reason my memories of family vacations are so memorable is because we took so few of them when I was growing up. I am convinced that sweets seldom received really are sweeter, and I have tried my best to raise my children not to be spoiled by too many rewards. The fact is, the few family vacations we took when I was young remain some of the most pleasant of all my memories.

Such was the case in my adolescence when we rolled into Carlsbad, New Mexico on our first trip to Carlsbad Caverns.

Actually, Carlsbad Caverns is really a misnomer. The Caverns are located in a park just outside a place called White's City. Carlsbad is a few miles away. I guess the National Park Service didn't think "White's City Caverns" had quite the same ring to it.

Anyway, the day we rolled into Carlsbad, they were doing construction on the stretch of highway between there and White's City. At 20 miles an hour, it seemed to take forever to travel the short distance.

Unlike most children, we did not verbalize the traditional "are we there yet?" on this trip, since our father had broken us of this habit long before. The first time we'd tried this on an earlier trip, my sister Glenda asked that very question. Dad responded with the answer "we'll be there in about ten minutes."

Of course, ten minutes came and went, as did the next hour. Glenda finally asked again: "Are we there yet?"

Dad's answer was the same, "we'll be there in about ten minutes."

When Glenda protested, "That's what you said last time, he retorted, "Well, I was wrong then. It'll be about ten minutes."

This went on a couple of more times, until it dawned on Glenda and the rest of us that regardless of how far away our destination was, we'd always get the same answer to our question. So we no longer bothered to ask.

Pretty clever, dad. I tried the same thing with my own children years later. It works. Try it.

Anyway, back to the caverns. We finally made it to White's City. I got the impression that whoever this White character was, he was a rich man. The White's City Motel was across the street from the White's City Souvenir Store, which was next door to the White's City Grocery and gas station.

Dad pulled into the gas station and saw the prices, and then pulled back out again. "I'll push this thing back to Carlsbad," he grumbled, "before I pay thirty cents a gallon."

The caverns were, in a word, spectacular. We started out by walking down a long winding path into the mouth of what looked like an ordinary cave. Once inside, we saw that this cave went on and on, as did the path which led us deeper and deeper inside the caverns.

All of the cavern's formations were impressive, although I was particularly struck by a rock formation that resembled an open shark's mouth, complete with teeth. I was fascinated by the stalactites and stalagmites, especially when the guide informed us that they had been formed over millions of years, by the mineral deposits in the water, dripping slowly from ceiling to floor. Very slowly, one drip, drip, drip at a time.

My favorite spot on the tour was called the "bottomless pit." The guide claimed that anyone falling into this pit would freefall forever. Of course, this was a slight exaggeration, but very believable to small boys. Especially since none of the people on the tour could see the bottom, despite several floodlights positioned with their bright lights shining deep into the hole.

I remember spending several minutes trying to entice my twin sister, Debbie, to the edge of the pit. For some inexplicable reason, she refused to trust me not to push her in. Like such a thought would ever cross my mind.

Having failed in the opportunity to toss Debbie into the abyss, I silently rejoined the group. We soon reached a huge cafeteria and souvenir shop at the bottom of the caverns, had some fried chicken, and rode the elevator a full two minutes to get back to the surface of the earth.

It was a pleasant experience, which I relived a few years ago with my own wife and children. I shouldn't have been, but I was amazed at how little it's changed after 30 years. The "bottomless pit" was still in the same spot. It brought a smile to my face as I thought of my sister Debbie.

My wife saw the smile on my face and gave me a peculiar look. Then she backed up a couple of steps and said "don't even think about it!"

Some things really never change.

Crooked Fingers

When I was a kid, people would ask me from time to time why my pinkies curve inward dramatically between the top and middle digits. Because I have always been slightly embarrassed to provide a truthful explanation, I usually used one of several made-up stories.

Back then, I told people that I broke both pinkies, and that they grew back improperly because the casts weren't applied correctly. For a boy, a broken bone is a badge of honor, a trophy to show off and brag about. Since I'd never broken any bones as a child, and was a bit jealous of my friends who had, I simply made up my own broken bones story.

For a long time, people seemed satisfied with my answer. Then one day an acquaintance made me pause to think when he said "Gee, how did you manage to break both pinkies at the same time?"

I could think of no plausible scenario for such an injury.

Then I started telling people that my curved pinkies were a hereditary thing. That was also an untruth. The fact is, my family members' pinkies might not be as straight as nails, but they weren't any more curved than anyone else's.

As a young boy, I had a terrible habit of popping my fingers. I did it constantly. Despite warnings from both of my parents and my grandmother that such a habit would lead to arthritis later in my life, I continued to pop my fingers several times a day.

I'm sure I irritated the heck out of my folks, but I didn't care. I guess that was my own personal rebellion against whatever was bugging me on any given day.

I learned early on that by tucking my pinky underneath the adjacent ring finger, and then pressing down on it with the top of my ring finger, I could pop the top digit of the pinky with one hand. This was an impressive feat for a six-year old. All of my friends used the traditional "two-handed" method to pop their finger joints.

After awhile, this became a habit, as natural to me as waking up each morning or grousing about going to school. Even later, it became so much of a habit that I found myself doing it without thinking.

By the time I noticed my pinkies were beginning to curve, it was too late to stop them.

Oh, I tried. For years, as a young adult, I twisted the top digit backwards, popping it toward the outside of my hand, in an effort to reverse the effect. Unfortunately, it did no good, and I've resigned myself to having permanently disfigured fingers.

This has been both an asset and a liability over the years. I've actually had women who took my hands in theirs, examined my fingers' rounded posture, and told me things like "oh, how cute…"

A living, breathing, conversation piece, that's what I was.

Conversely, my inability to use all of my fingers independently resulted in my being the only student in my high school freshman class who failed typing class. As a fledgling journalist, this should have been almost a prerequisite, but I learned that first year in high school that I could never learn to type like everyone else. My pinkies simply weren't straight enough to hit their assigned keys. Instead, they would invariably hit two keys at once.

To this day, I type using three fingers: two on my right hand and my left index finger. Still, at 40 words a minute, I do a pretty good job of cranking out the text.

I also noticed long ago that this condition affects the way I hold a baseball bat and a golf club, since my pinkies get in the way when I grip something tightly. For that reason, I've developed a habit of sticking my pinky out, in the same way an Englishman holds his teacup when he's sharing tea time with aristocratic snobs.

As far as I know, this method of holding a bat and a club hasn't affected my playing ability. I can still strike out or shank a drive with the best of them.

I've been careful to watch my own children and grandchildren very closely over the years to ensure they don't repeat my mistake. So far, so good.

Other than being a source of amusement for others, and slowing down my typing a bit, my bent fingers haven't had an adverse affect on my life. A friend once asked me if I'd ever considered having plastic surgery to correct the problem. I replied that they weren't really much of a problem. If I ever have so much money burning a hole in my pocket that I feel a need for cosmetic surgery, I'll spend it on hair transplants instead.

The Uniform

These days, it's hard to find a resident of Lubbock, Texas who isn't a Dallas Cowboys fan. Since my home town doesn't have a professional football team of its own it, like most other cities and towns in the area, has adopted the Cowboys as its unofficial "home team." Consequently, on any given Sunday afternoon during football season, an exceedingly large percentage of households in Lubbock have their televisions tuned into the Cowboys game. When the team does well, Cowboys mania overtakes the whole region.

This wasn't always the case.

When the Cowboys franchise first started out in 1960, they didn't win many of their games. In fact, it took them several seasons to build a team that was both talented and reliable.

Since the Cowboys' success was slow in coming, so was their following.

Prior to the famous "Ice Bowl" championship game against the Green Bay Packers, there were many people in west Texas who still weren't aware that Dallas even had a professional football team.

Even though the championship game, set in sub-zero temperatures in Green Bay, is now renowned as one of football history's defining moments, the bottom line feeling in Lubbock after it was over was that the Cowboys blew the game.

Actually, the Cowboys put up a good fight. With a young team, and coaches with limited experience, they were just outplayed that particular day. If the weather had been more friendly that day to a visiting team unused to such frigid conditions, they might have been victorious. On this particular day, though, the Packers, coached by the legendary Vince Lombardi, was simply the better team.

Considering the sentiment involved at the time, it wasn't surprising when, at his birthday party a few weeks later, my friend Mark received a bright and shiny new Green Bay

Packer helmet, gold in color with an elongated letter "G" on both sides. It looked exactly like the helmet the real Packers wore when we saw them play on television.

Since we all had black and white television sets, this was the first time we'd ever seen this helmet in color, and it was a sight to behold. Mark was the immediate envy of all the boys at his birthday party. The helmet was passed around the room, as each boy fought for his turn to try it on.

Mark opened another box, and a hush fell across the room. He pulled out a gold pair of football pants and a green jersey, also exact replicas of the uniform the Packers wore. The number on the jersey, 15, was the number of the one and only Bart Starr, the quarterback who led the Packers during their glory years. And who ran the winning touchdown that beat the Cowboys in the ice bowl.

Anyone who knew Mark back then knew that Bart Starr was Mark's hero. His bedroom wall was plastered with Packers pennants and Bart Starr posters, and any time we played football he insisted on being the quarterback.

To add the finishing touches, Mark's parents also gave him a pair of shoulder pads and rubber cleats. My other friends and I were "Packer" green with envy.

The party effectively ended when Mark opened the last of the boxes. The cake would have to wait, and there would be no more celebrating. It was time to get outside and play some football.

As impressive as Mark looked in his new uniform, it certainly didn't help his game any. The playground at P.F. Brown Elementary School was pretty barren, and since spring had not yet started to change brown things to green, what little grass existed was as dead as could be.

We found that Mark's hard rubber cleats were made to dig into soft grass, and were absolutely worthless on hard, bare ground. While Mark the quarterback was running around the backfield, trying to avoid being tackled while his receivers were getting open, he was slipping and sliding and finding it harder to stay on his feet. Even worse, his heavy pads slowed him down to such a degree that it was easy for the defenders to catch him and grind him into the dirt.

His helmet didn't fit either. About two sizes too large for his head, it flopped around when he ran, like it was balanced on the top of a moving broomstick. The chinstrap did little good. Any time Mark turned his head, the helmet stayed more or less in place, doing a pretty effective job of obscuring his vision.

As good as Mark looked in his new uniform, he finally decided that it was worthless in a game of sandlot football when his opponents weren't slowed down by the same type of gear. First the helmet came off, then the shoulder pads. Finally, he took off his shiny new cleats and played barefoot.

I've known Mark for many years since that football game, but I never again saw him wear that uniform. He hung the jersey on his bedroom wall, and the helmet from his light fixture, and they stayed there for a long time.

Eventually Mark, like virtually everyone else in that part of Texas, became a Cowboys fan, and the Packers gear was discarded. Although it didn't get a lot of wear, it did serve its purpose. It taught Mark and the rest of us that clothes do not make the man, and a fancy uniform does not make a good ballplayer.

Football

My first experience with organized sports came when I was in sixth grade at P. F. Brown Elementary School. An announcement came crackling over the public address box in Mr. Bowling's classroom one morning, announcing tryouts that afternoon for the school football team. I decided then and there that I would become an athlete.

"Tryouts" was probably a misnomer, since there were so few boys interested that everyone made the team. After the coach took down all the players' names, we ran a few drills so that the coach and his two assistants could determine where best to place their new charges.

I became a "receiver." Not a tight end, not a wide receiver, just a receiver. This, according to the coach, meant that I didn't have a permanent spot to line up at the beginning of each play. I could stand anywhere I wanted behind the line of scrimmage, and between the offensive line and the sideline.

My instructions once the ball was snapped were equally vague. No post or slant or lateral patterns for me. I was told only to "get open every play."

We were easily the most disorganized team in football. Although we were having fun, and occasionally even showed a spark of talent, we had no aspirations of winning any championships. Or ball games, for that matter.

Our first game was at Roscoe Wilson Elementary. Our coach kept calling the school "our rival," and we took his word for that, since none of us had ever heard of them before the game.

We played using only the basic, rudimentary equipment: no pads, no cleats, just a beat up and scarred helmet and a brown jersey, and whatever shoes we happened to wear to school that day.

These days, playing tackle football without the latest hi-tech pads and helmets would cause many parents to threaten lawsuits as they dragged junior off the field and into the mini-van. Back then, we didn't care, and neither did our folks. We just wanted to play ball, and would have played in our pajamas if we were asked to. Our parents just wanted us to get out of the house for a bit.

As I recall, Roscoe Wilson played quite well. They had some actual plays. Everyone had an assignment, and went to a specific place each play. None of them stumbled over each other, as our team did.

Although I was able to "get open" quite frequently, I was seldom thrown the ball, since our quarterback was almost always buried under a pile of defenders by that time.

I did, however, make a couple of catches. Nothing spectacular, and I didn't, as I had dreamed the night before, break a tackle and scamper for a touchdown.

I can't recall the final score, but we were beaten pretty badly. It seemed to bother the coach much more than it bothered us. After all, win or lose, we were having a blast. The coach, on the other hand, told us we were going to drive him to drink if we didn't shape up.

Before the next game, we spent a lot of time practicing the "fundamentals." That was the coach's term, not ours, and it basically meant we ran and blocked and tackled until we couldn't run and block and tackle anymore.

Losing our first game also meant changes to our game plan, and everyones' assignments changed. First, I was to block somebody on every play. Then I was to get open. The intent, as I understood it, was to help keep the defenders from getting to the quarterback so quickly. I suppose it worked, because he seemed to have more time to throw the ball. He needed the extra time, because blocking the defenders also meant it took longer for his receivers to get open. Nobody wanted to point this out to the coach.

We lost the second game by three touchdowns, on our home field. Not a good way to show off to the girls in the crowd.

For our third game we worked on our running attack. Our biggest players were shifted to the offensive line, and told to shove the defensive players to one side each play so that our running back could run through the hole. This actually worked to some degree, and we actually managed to win the game.

Since our ground game had worked and our passing game hadn't, I spent most of the rest of the season "getting open," then turning around and walking back to the huddle. Not a dazzling start to my athletic career, which is probably the reason I never became a superstar in the National Football League. If only they'd thrown me the ball more, who knows where I might have gone?

Shirley Ann

Most of us wonder from time to time what became of our past loves or acquaintances. I'm no different. I've done it a lot more over the past few years, because as I've gotten older I've spent a lot more time exorcizing the demons of my past, and reliving the happy times of my youth.

I recently moved from Atlanta to San Antonio, Texas. It's actually the second time I've lived in this beautiful and unique city. Parts of my teenage years were spent here, and one of the first things I did after I arrived was to spend a day driving around, revisiting all the places I'd remembered from my past.

I started by revisiting the houses I'd lived in as a teenager. As I suspected, this exercise brought back a rush of memories, and reliving them was a thoroughly enjoyable experience.

I also visited the Dwight Middle School and South San Antonio High School campuses. Despite renovations at both schools, and the addition of some troubling reminders that my old neighborhoods had deteriorated a bit, like graffiti, front yard fences and barbed wire, I enjoyed rewalking the halls and grounds where I had spent a good portion of my youth.

It was after I left South San High, and was driving down Southcross Street, that I remembered that Shirley Ann Gandera once lived in this neighborhood. I wondered, could she still be there?

Shirley Ann was one of my first loves. We were introduced by my twin sister Debbie after church one day. Almost immediately we started spending time together after services on the church steps, not far from the Alamo.

I think what attracted me to Shirley Ann initially was her willingness to sit and talk for hours at a time about our hopes and dreams and plans for the future. Of course, the fact that she was drop-dead gorgeous didn't hurt any either. I would gaze into her soft brown eyes, brush the silky-black hair away from her face, and explain to her how I felt the weight of the whole world upon my shoulders.

She listened patiently and helped me realize that no problem was insurmountable, and helped me work through whatever it was that was bothering me on that particular day. I did the same for her. In a sense, we became soul mates. Then we experimented, as youngsters do at that age, with kissing and holding hands, and holding each other tightly to guard against the chill of the night.

Clearly, we had fallen in love, although we never professed those feelings to each other. It was enough, it seemed, just to be there for one another.

I remember one night in particular, sitting on the steps of the church long after everyone had gone home, trying to imagine our world decades later. We laughed aloud as we tried to guess where we'd be, and what we'd be doing, and how many kids we'd have. We spoke of a single future, taking it for granted that we'd always be together. The children weren't "your kids" or "my kids," they were "our kids," and we envisioned them all breaking the binds of poverty and becoming successful doctors, lawyers and industry giants.

Our evenings always ended in the same manner, with a soft goodnight kiss, a lingering hug, and a smile that said what mere words couldn't.

One of the great tragedies of my life is that Shirley Ann and I never had a chance to say goodbye. The turmoil that was my life back then was such that one day without warning I was whisked away and taken back to Lubbock, where I'd been born some 15 years before. As we always do when special things end without proper closure, I mourned the fact that Shirley Ann was no longer in my life. I'd never again be able to lose myself in those beautiful brown eyes. I'd never again feel her touch, or taste her kiss, or experience the joy of her laughter.

What I missed more than anything, though, was the way she always seemed to know what I was thinking, as though we were one. Even though the words "I love you" never crossed our lips, that bond was unmistakably there and understood by both of us. The reason it went unsaid wasn't because we were afraid of the words or what they meant. There simply was no need to express how we both obviously felt.

I've wondered many times over the years what happened to Shirley Ann. The Gandera family long ago moved from the neighborhood. No one who lives there now knows who they are or where they went.

I once searched the phone book looking for Shirley Ann's name. Of course I found no such listing. I knew it was a long shot, for there's no way that my raven-haired beauty wouldn't have been married and changed her name long before. Still, something inside me told me I had to try.

Shirley Ann once told me that she wanted to be a pediatrician when she finished medical school. Watching her with small children convinced me that she'd be good at it, for she not only loved life, but loved life's littlest creatures most of all. I hope she was able to realize that particular dream. In fact, I hope all her dreams came true. If there is a God and a heaven above, and if I ever make it there, I hope that Shirley Ann and I can spend part of eternity sharing happy moments from our respective pasts. It'll be just like old times...

Cop Cars and Fishing Line

My dad once told my little brother Randy and I about some pranks he pulled when he was a kid. At the time, I was about ten or so, and Randy was two years younger than me. To this day I still don't know if Dad was just making conversation, or was giving us hints about fun things to do on a boring summer day.

I remember that one prank in particular got our attention, and we immediately knew we had to try it. Randy and I took the idea and ran with it, right down the street to Kent's house. Then we told Dennis, and we were set.

Dad had told how he and his brothers would take one of their mom's old purses, tie a length of heavy fishing line to it, and leave it by the side of the highway near my great-granddad's old farm in Tahoka, Texas.

The boys would hide in a large culvert that went under the road, about 30 yards from the purse, with the other end of the fishing line.

Fishing line, as you can probably guess, is darned hard to spot when you're driving down a lonely stretch of highway at 60 miles an hour. But, not so surprisingly, an abandoned purse gets a lot of attention.

Since this was a country highway without a lot of traffic, my dad and his brothers sometimes had to wait several minutes between cars. Eventually, though, they'd hear a car coming, and would crouch down low to watch the action.

Sure enough, a car would come speeding by and the driver would spot the purse and slam on his brakes. The boys would take that as their cue to reel in their purse as fast as they could. By the time the driver backed up to the spot where he or she saw the purse, it was long gone.

My dad roared with laughter as he told of the drivers who would get out of their cars, scratch their heads, and search for long periods for the purse. They no doubt left some poor souls doubting their own sanity. But Dad said they only got caught a couple of times. And they apparently provided some entertainment for the local farmers.

He said the farmers working in their fields would stop their tractors and harvesters and take a break while they watched the drivers search in vain for the mysterious vanishing purse, probably laughing their asses off all the while.

Dad said that after awhile the fun wore off, because word got around not to stop and pick up womens' purses on the Tahoka Highway. Randy and I and our buddies noticed the same thing. After we pulled this stunt several times over the course of the summer on the street in front of our houses, we noticed that after awhile, people stopped stopping.

We then came up with a new prank, which came dangerously close to getting us into a world of trouble. It was Kent's idea, as I recall. "You know," he said, "this fishing line's pretty strong stuff. I'll bet if we tied each end to an empty trash can, and strung it across the alley, that a car coming through there would hit it, and the trash cans would bang both car doors."

We looked at each other and smiled. It just might work.

Now, these trash cans weren't the wimpy plastic kitchen variety we all know and use today. These were 50-gallon, galvanized steel suckers that shone like new silver dollars in the sunlight, and easily weighed thirty pounds each. They had handles riveted into each side just about headlight-high, perfect for tying fishing line onto.

The first time we set up the line, we waited forty-five minutes for the first car to come through, and cursed as the car cut the line on its grill. That led to some heavier fishing line, and a very long wait for the next car.

After what seemed like hours, we heard a car coming up the alley, and took safe refuge behind the fence in our back yard. We watched through the slats of the fence, and turned a ghostly white when we saw the police car doing its routine patrol through the alley, getting ever closer to our fishing line.

This was the only time I can remember wanting one of our pranks not to work. But it worked perfectly. The police car hit the fishing line strung across the alley about eighteen inches off the ground. The line tightened and pulled the metal trash cans in from each side of the alley. The next thing we heard was a loud "wham!" as both trash cans hit the front doors of the police car at the same time.

We never saw the policeman get out of the car, though. We never saw the look on his face, or heard the profanity he probably hurled at us. By the time the policeman got out of the car, we were miles away. We were looking over our shoulders for several days. And no, we never pulled that particular stunt again. But I always wanted to. And I do have some 30 pound test line out in the utility room...

Gym Class

It takes a special breed of person to rule a junior high school gymnasium. Take one part history teacher, one part assistant football coach, and one part sadist, and you have a perfect gym teacher.

You're careful to call him "coach," because you know if you forget and call him "mister," you'll spend the afternoon running laps.

He's a man who is an expert at finding your weaknesses and pointing them out to the entire class. A man whose entire vocabulary consists of catch-phrases he picked up from old movies about athletic events.

"C'mon, kid," he'd say when I missed an easy layup on the basketball court. "You're letting down your team. Get your head up and the lead out and win one for the Gipper..."

I was not particularly athletic when I was a kid. I was no worse than most of the kids I hung around with, but I didn't have to worry about turning the heads of any scouts at the football game, either.

Unless, of course, I spilled my drink on them as I fought my way to my seat.

Gym teachers, as I said, have a knack for finding every kid's weakness and ridiculing them about it. In my case, it was a lack of upper arm strength. As a kid, I was painfully skinny. My arms were like toothpicks, and could barely lift the combined weight of my hands and whatever they happened to be carrying at any particular moment. So when I walked into the gym one spring day and saw a long rope hanging from the ceiling to the floor, I felt a particular queasiness in the pit of my stomach.

I knew what was coming. "All right," Coach Phillips began, to the dismay of most of the class. "It's the last inning of the big game, and everybody's tired. So how do we know who's gonna win the game? Easy! The team who digs the deepest, the team who's the strongest, will be the team that ends up with the trophy. Let's go get 'em, boys!"

We sat confused, trying to figure out what a fifty foot length of rope had to do with winning a baseball game.

Nobody moved, until the coach yelled again. "I said move it, boys! The clock is ticking!" We lined up in a pitiful queue, staring up at the ceiling and wondering how much it was going to hurt when we lost our grip and hit the gym floor from such a great height. Which of us would be the first to die?

"Move it! You're lolly-gagging around like a bunch of girls!" Coach Phillips had such a way with words. None of us knew what a lolly was, or what gagging it would do. But we knew we'd be running laps if we didn't move, so we did.

Probably half the class was able to climb to the top of the gym, slap the rafter, and shimmy back down. I did it, although with considerable difficulty. "What's taking you so long, Maloney?" The coach's words echoed across the expanse of the gymnasium. "You're chewing up what's left on the game clock!"

Getting down, of course, was much easier than going up. Much faster, too, since most of us slid down the last few feet to get the coach off our backs. Then we stomped around the gym cursing under our breath because of the blisters the rope burn left on our hands.

I was more fortunate than some. Wesley could barely get his feet off the floor. He finally climbed up about three feet, and hung there, like a man clinging to life from the hundredth floor of a high-rise.

Try as he might, he couldn't budge another inch, not even when Coach Phillips let loose a barrage of obscenities and openly questioned Wesley's true gender.

Being called a sissy often motivated young boys of my generation into taking stupid dares. But it was not possible to insult a body into doing something it was not equipped to do. Coach Phillips eventually gave up on Wesley and told him to hit the showers, warning him that he had two weeks to get into shape before the next rope drill.

We spent the next two weeks doing intense weight training to build up our upper bodies. The coach had a point he wanted to make. He said when we identified a particular weakness, we were to work on that weakness until we were able to "conquer our demons." After all, he repeatedly told us, "The game could be riding on it..."

For two long weeks we wrestled barbells in the weight room. Then we once again lined up under the rope. To set the stage for what he expected was a dramatic improvement in everyones' climbing ability, the coach singled out Wesley and reminded everyone how this weakling could barely clear the floor the first time we'd assembled there.

"Now watch the difference," he said as he gazed at us. Back to Wesley, he barked an order. "Now get up that damn rope!"

Wesley would claim later that he repeated his earlier performance just to embarrass the coach. I never knew whether to believe him or not. What was certain, however, was that Wesley would climb no further up the rope than he'd gone two weeks before. Despite all the weight training and all the belittling, Wesley's feet topped out about eighteen inches off the floor and hung there.

After a stream of heavy duty cursing that would make any sailor blush, Coach Phillips ordered Wesley off the rope and told everyone to stand back.

"I'm going to show you how it's supposed to be done."

Now, no one assembled in the gym that particular morning wished any ill will toward the coach, except maybe Wesley, but he had a right to.

However, we all secretly wished he be unable to climb to the top of the rope, so that somehow we'd be vindicated. We figured we deserved that much for the abuse we'd been taking.

But Coach Phillips had the arm strength of a gorilla, and deftly climbed the rope in record time, slapped the rafter at the top of the gym, and climbed back down. Everything went well until he was about twenty feet from the floor. Then, with a sickening snap, the swivel hook which fastened the rope to the ceiling gave way, and the coach came crashing to the floor.

The man we'd come to despise was not seriously hurt. But he did fracture his tail bone, which we thought was a fitting punishment. He took a week off after the fall, and then walked funny for the rest of the school year. In our minds, justice was aptly served. The rope was never rehung. We spent the rest of the school year playing basketball, and not worrying about how strong our upper bodies were. Karma is our friend. Yes, indeed...

The Great Trash Robbery of 1968

Carlisle Park was just six short blocks from my house in Lubbock when I was a kid. It was a typical suburban street park, spanning 150 yards in length, and about 80 yards in width.

It was landscaped sporadically with a smattering of brush, tall trees, and playground equipment. Just east of the center of the park, facing to the west, was a recreational building. It was a moderately-sized brick structure consisting of restrooms for boys and girls, a "pool room," which contained not billiard tables, but chlorine and swimming pool equipment, an office for park staff, and a "game room."

From the game room on summer mornings came a wide assortment of board games, ping pong tables, carom tables, and sporting equipment to occupy the time of dozens of neighborhood children needing things to do during their summer vacation.

Behind the structure, in the southeast corner of the park, was a shallow in-ground wading pool, barely 18 inches at its deepest point, but capable of holding enough water to keep everyone cool when the temperature topped 100 degrees, which it frequently does in Lubbock during the summer months.

A staff of three Texas Tech University students, employed for the summer, organized games and activities to keep their young charges out of mischief and involved in wholesome pursuits.

Collectively, these things served to make summer considerably more enjoyable for my friends and I as I grew.

One summer when I was about 10, the staff decided that the park was getting too messy, and declared that they would hold a "litter pickup contest." They called all the stray boys and girls together, passed out plastic bags, and announced the rules: they'd blow the whistle to start the event, give everyone twenty minutes to pick up litter inside the park, and blow the whistle again to end the contest. Simple enough.

They promised a prize to the boy and girl with the fullest bags. The whistle blew, and off we scampered in all directions.

Most of the litter, we knew, had blown into a wall of shrubs at the west end of the park, on the other side of the tennis and shuffleboard courts. That's where Wesley Scoggins, Ronnie Roscoe and I went, along with most of the other kids.

Twenty minutes later, after clawing through the bushes collecting paper, old soda pop bottles (they didn't always come in cans), and other assorted garbage, we heard the whistle blow again at the other end of the park. We were scratched up and filthy, but fairly confident from the mass of litter we had collected that we each had a good chance of winning.

Ronnie and I had about the same amount of trash, and Wesley had a huge piece of cardboard stuffed into his bag that made it look like he'd collected more than he really did.

He was hoping that if they didn't look too closely, that he might take home the prize. All participants reassembled in front of the recreation building.

Out of nowhere came Kent Dobkins, who didn't go with us into the stand of bushes. Kent was dragging a bag so bursting with trash that it made everyone else's' hauls look absurdly anorexic.

Had the park staff peered closer into Kent's bag, they'd have seen some items that might have looked familiar to them. Luckily for him they didn't.

After he accepted his prize and the crowd broke up, Kent shared his secret for success with us. Amidst all the chaos, he'd simply sneaked into the girls' restroom and dumped the garbage can into his bag. He did the same in the boys' restroom. Then he snuck into the staff's office and took their trash as well.

Absolutely brilliant. Kent's prize was a football. It was used, and probably would have been thrown away, since the park had just bought two new footballs to replace the old ones. But we hadn't had a football to play with in awhile, since Matthew Hanson left his in his front yard one night several months earlier and it was stolen. So used or not, it was a suitable prize that would provide us with many hours of enjoyment.

I cannot remember what prize was given to the girl who won her division. I suppose that shouldn't concern me, since at the time I couldn't have cared less.

As I recall, we played with that old football until eventually the seam came apart and the black rubber bladder began to peek out from between the pieces of leather. If you've never seen a football in this condition, rest assured it tests your ability to throw a perfect spiral when the ball has a large black air bubble clinging to its side. Kent's stunt became known in our circle as "the great trash robbery," and we laughed about it for years.

I think the park staff eventually realized they'd been had, since that was the one and only time they ever held a litter collecting contest.

Carlisle Park still sits in the same spot today, at the corner of 27th Street and Avenue W, a few blocks due south of Chapman Field. It's changed a lot, though. The wading pool, the recreation building, the tennis courts, and many of the trees and shrubs are now gone. Where the recreation building once stood, there now sits a boring, generic piece of playground equipment.

Last time I was in Lubbock I stopped by this park, sat under a tall elm tree, and watched a new generation of kids playing at the park. It saddened me that they had missed the park's glory days, when the city spent much more time, effort and money on their parks, and actually made them fun places for kids to spend their time.

I know those days are gone forever, yet I'm glad that I had the opportunity to experience the place when it was really something to enjoy. I hope I'm not the only one to remember this park the way it once was. If anyone else does, please drop me a line. We've got a lot of memories to share.

Flower Children and Peace Signs

I led a sheltered life growing up. There was so much going on in the world in the mid-1960s that I was simply not aware of. I was so caught up in my own little piece of the world that I completely missed Vietnam, Woodstock, the peace demonstrations, and the civil rights movement.

I remember JFK's funeral only because it was the first time I saw my mother cry.

One thing I did experience, although I didn't understand at the time that they were a national phenomenon, and didn't even know they had a name associated with them, were "hippies."

Don't get me wrong. It wasn't like Lubbock, Texas was overrun with flower children. In my neighborhood, the extent of our hippie infestation was one house around the corner on 31st Street. This house, which was painted canary yellow with purple trim (which even *I* thought was ugly at the time) was home to fifteen or so young men and women, in traditional hippie garb: bell-bottomed jeans of all colors, tie-dyed t-shirts, wide leather belts with peace symbols as belt buckles. Halter tops and cut-off jeans for the girls, and long stringy hair of equal length for both sexes.

We didn't have a clue who these people were or what they represented. All we knew was they looked odd to us, and provided free entertainment.

Their house was on our way to Carlisle Park, which we frequented almost daily during the hot summer months. I remember the group as being friendly and well-mannered, always smiling and waving to us as we walked or rode by on our bicycles. They frequently asked us to stop and visit with them, and were always quick to offer something cold to drink, or fresh baked cookies or fruit.

One girl of 19 or 20 with long blonde hair used to sit on a chair under the tree in the front yard strumming away on a guitar. Often she sang songs, and occasionally her friends joined in and sang with her. On these occasions, we sat in the grass and listened. I suppose that this was partly because she was young and pretty. Also, someone sitting in their yard singing and playing a guitar was something we didn't see every day. It was unique and interesting. And even fun.

I don't remember these hippies ever causing any problems at all. In this very conservative neighborhood, I knew that some of the neighbors didn't want them around. But these same neighbors probably didn't go sit on their grass with them and listen to their music and try to get to know them either.

I remember occasionally hearing some of the adults on my street complain about them, as though they were somehow a menace to the neighborhood or to our way of life.

As a kid, I knew to keep my opinions to myself, but I couldn't quite understand exactly what the grownups had against these people. Looking back, I'm convinced that these hippies could come back and teach the world a few things.

During the two or three years I remember them living there, I can't recall ever seeing any of them argue. When they had something to do, like fix someone's car or clean or mow the yard, they pitched in together and swarmed over the project like a bunch of busy ants. Teamwork in action.

Best of all, they let my friends and I watch, and sometimes even help, without being judgmental and assuming that because we were kids we had nothing to say or contribute.

One day we passed by the house and they were gone. We never had a chance to say goodbye to them, and it probably never occurred to them to tell us they were leaving. I remember feeling a little sad, suspecting that I would never meet anyone like them again. Our one and only encounter with hippies was over.

Within a couple of weeks, the house was repainted a conservative gray color, and not long after that an older couple moved in.

Occasionally I'll see film footage on TV about Woodstock, and I'll scan the crowds looking for the blonde girl or another familiar face. Perhaps that's where they went when they left.

Or perhaps they determined that our neighborhood didn't want them, and moved on to another place that might welcome their peculiar habits.

For a long time, I've believed that ultra-conservative Lubbock was out of touch with the rest of the country. It's always been a city with twice as many churches as bars, uptight snooty people who'd just as soon turn up their noses as say hello to a stranger, and media which railed frequently and loudly against anything that went against their ultra-conservative, uber-religious beliefs.

For a long time, you couldn't go into a supermarket on a Sunday and expect to buy anything other than groceries. Blue laws required stores to rope off anything that was not edible, as though buying flashlight batteries on a Sunday was a direct violation of God's eleventh commandment.

It was only last year that Lubbock finally started allowing sales of beer and wine inside the city limits. Before that time one had to drive outside the city to buy a can of Bud Light. Really. Lubbock has never been the kind of place that welcomed strangers, especially those who looked or acted differently. I suspect that the hippies left, at least in part, because their neighbors couldn't bring themselves to adjust to a changing world.

As far as I was concerned, they were a good group of people. I missed them for a long time. And every time I've driven past that house in the years since then, I've thought about how much better it looked when it was bright yellow.

Grandma's Basement

In a little house on Colgate Street in my hometown of Lubbock, Texas, there is a basement that is home to the ghosts of Billy the Kid, the great warrior Sitting Bull, and Blackbeard the pirate. Really.

This was the house where my Grandma Maloney lived when I was a small boy. She seldom went down into the basement, so it was essentially the domain of my brother and I most of the time. Except for Sundays.

Across the street from Grandma's house was the Colgate Street Church of Christ, where our family went each Sunday morning. It was our weekly opportunity to see our cousins from across town, since my uncles Glen and Bob and their families attended services at the same church.

After church services were over each Sunday, all of my relatives gathered at Grandma's house, where the adults would sit around the living room to visit, and the kids would all assemble in the back yard or basement.

The adults would talk about who died the previous week, who was in the hospital, and generally gossip about friends and fellow churchgoers.

The kids had much more fun.

Just off the basement, immediately adjacent to an old, creaky set of wooden stairs, was a small closet which contained a water heater. This water heater had seen better times. Years of heating water, letting out excess steam, and pumping the water to various locations throughout the house had taken its toll on this antiquated appliance. It produced a variety of noises, ranging from hissing sounds, to creaking, to an occasional mournful groan.

For years, my siblings and cousins and I refused to enter the small closet to investigate the noises. We took it for granted that the closet was home to several ghosts, and since they didn't bother us, we went about our business of playing.

Over time we'd learned, although I can't remember exactly how, the names of the ghosts. It seems pretty incredible now that such famous spirits as those of Billy the Kid, Sitting Bull and Blackbeard, would congregate for eternity in the basement of this nondescript little house. But in the minds of young children, things like that happen without rhyme or reason every day. Besides, as I've often said, kids never let things like logic get in the way of their fantasies.

The basement was far from watertight, and its walls were frequently damp for days after a good rainstorm. This contributed to a deep smell of mildew and discolored walls, and gave the basement the eerie feel of a mad scientist's laboratory.

Of course, the moist air meant that the basement was always the coolest part of the house, even on the hottest of summer days. While dad and his brothers were upstairs tinkering with Grandma's swamp cooler, trying to milk just a little bit more cool air from it, we were hidden from view, calm, cool and content.

There were times, though, when the moist basement air didn't seem so friendly. When the humidity was just right, and the temperature was in the right range, there would actually be fog in the basement. The fog, in our minds, were the ghosts that had gotten out of the closet and were walking around the basement looking for us. On those days, we stayed out of the basement altogether and played outside instead.

My brother and I thought we invented the game of handball. We used an old "Super-ball" and bounced it off the concrete walls of Grandma's basement for hours at a time, taking turns hitting it with our open hands. Randy almost always trounced me, since he was smaller and faster than me. It wasn't until years later that I found out fitness clubs had special courts built to play the same game we used to play as children.

In the corner of the basement was an old couch and a couple of folding chairs. The couch had absorbed the same dank smell as the rest of the basement, and was therefore permanently rendered unusable by polite company. For us kids, though, it was just a big, soft though smelly, place to sit and catch our breath.

Adjacent to the couch was a stack of old comic books, torn and tattered, with black spots of mildew on some of the pages. Dad periodically threw them out and replaced them with a fresh stack from old man Scott's used book store. I think he did it to keep us in the basement as much as possible.

Sometimes we'd get bored and roll balls down the old wooden steps. We'd make a game of who could make the ball bounce the greatest number of times before it made contact with the basement floor. This led to some ingenious techniques of launching the ball, including applying backspin to it, and banking it several times off the walls. Inadvertently, we probably learned a lot about physics on those steps without really intending to. I still hold the record, by the way.

The basement was extremely comforting, almost a home away from home. About the only time I was ever uncomfortable there was one rainy Sunday afternoon, when a bad thunderstorm blew in and Grandma's lights went out for a few minutes.

While we were sitting in the dark, telling ghost stories, the door to the water heater closet suddenly opened. We couldn't see it, but the slow creaking sound was unmistakable. It was as though the ghostly residents wanted to join us. I can still recall the hair on the back of my neck standing on end.

For a long time after that we refused to go into the basement. On good weather days we'd play in the backyard. On cold or rainy days, we'd sit on the basement steps and talk and look nervously at the dark room at the foot of the stairs.

We told the grownups about the closet door, but of course none of them believed us. Eventually we mustered up the courage to return to the basement, and we examined the door thoroughly. We tried to understand what would make it open on its own at that particular moment in time. We never did figure it out.

Grandma died many years ago, and the old house belongs to someone else now. Someday I'd like to walk up to the door and ask if I can step into that dark, damp basement one last time. I'd like to see if Billy, the Chief, and Blackbeard are still there.

On second thought, maybe I shouldn't. The power might go out again…

Mercado Juarez

I guess my first trip outside the United States would have been much more exciting if I had known at the time what the United States were and what it meant to leave them. I'd just turned six years old when, as part of a summer vacation trip, my family drove into El Paso, Texas. From there we drove across the International Bridge into Juarez, Mexico.

Many aspects of the trip are fuzzy. It has been a few years, after all. I remember going to a small city park with an ancient fountain, and children my age playing in the water. Some of them were naked, which both shocked me a bit and also struck me as funny. That vision stuck in my memory, I suppose, because I remember it being miserably hot. I would have loved to have joined the children, although we had no bathing suits, but we weren't allowed to.

Instead, we ate lunch, and bought some ice cream from an old vendor pushing a large two-wheeled cart through the park.

There seemed to be a fiesta of some sort going on. There was music wafting through the park, and pretty dancing girls, and I remember the locals being dressed in traditional Mexican garb. The men all wore sombreros, the women wore scarves of many colors. Whatever was going on, everyone was enjoying it tremendously.

After leaving the park, my next memory is of parking the car on a crowded street. I seem to recall it taking my father an extremely long time to find a parking place, finally wedging the big station wagon between a lamp post and a car with a flat tire. From there, we walked through the hustle and bustle of crowded streets and alleys to the mercado, or market.

The Mercado Juarez took up an entire city block and, luckily, was air conditioned. I suppose that was to discourage the shoppers from leaving too soon. Every inch of floor space was occupied with vendors selling their wares. It very closely resembled a modern day flea market, except that none of the vendors spoke any English.

Other than the chaotic nature of the market, the thing I remember the most was the fresh fruit vendor in the center of the building. I remember him in particular because he encouraged us to sample everything he had. We happily did this, and I remember eating my fill of grapes, strawberries and bright red cherries. We washed the fruit down with Nehi Orange and Coca-Cola, from glass bottles that were slightly smaller than their U.S. counterparts.

The only other thing I remember about the Juarez market was an old Mexican puppet my parents bought me. Carved out of wood, and painted in brilliant colors, the little man danced at the end of six strings, which were secured to two wooden crossed sticks.

I didn't play with the puppet much, because it just wasn't as interesting as my G.I. Joe or Matchbox cars, but for a long time it occupied space on the wall of my bedroom. I haven't got a clue what happened to the puppet. The little old man was discarded, given away, or lost long ago.

I often go back to the places I traveled in my youth. Just as stories of days gone by jar new memories from the recesses of my mind, so too does revisiting old houses, neighborhoods, schools and businesses I used to frequent. That's why, when I lived in Alamogordo a few years ago, I heard Juarez singing my name, calling me to come back for a visit.

This time I walked across the bridge into Mexico, leaving my car behind because I'd heard that theft of tourists' cars was now a major problem.

The streets of Juarez were the same: colorful, crowded and festive. I immediately noticed a proliferation of beggars that I didn't remember from before: crippled old men and children in ragged clothing with pitiful looks on their faces.

I never found the park, although I'm sure it's still there somewhere, unchanged in the last fifty years. It turns out the Mercado is one of the biggest tourist attractions in the city, and I had had absolutely no trouble finding it.

As I walked through the door, the air conditioning hit me like a ton of bricks. In that instant, I regressed in age. I was a little boy again, and everywhere I looked I saw things that brought back memories of the first time I'd been there.

The medium brown plaster on the walls, the crowded shops, the floor worn down from decades of ceaseless foot traffic; it was all exactly the same as I'd seen it before.

The fruit stand still sits in the middle of the market, although I was unable to talk the vendor out of any free samples. The puppets were all over the place, and they looked exactly as I remembered them. Coca Cola is still sold in glass bottles, and there is still a festive atmosphere about the place.

About the only thing that's changed is now all the vendors speak English at least as well as you and I do.

My sons Chris and Justin went with me on the trip. They appeared to have a reasonably good time. I hope it was enjoyable enough to make them want to make a return trip someday. If they do, I hope that the city doesn't change a bit.

I suspect it never will.

Summer of '71

Few things fascinate adolescent boys as much as new homes or businesses under construction. There's just something about the process of creating a structure where only dirt and grass existed before that appeals to every boy, in the same way building a house of playing cards or something with an erector set does. Boys in general, I think, love to take things apart, just so they can put them back together again. They love to see things materialize from nothing.

In my retirement years, I've chosen to live in San Antonio, Texas. Although I've lived in or visited all of the United States, I've never found a more beautiful city. The Alamo City is rich in historical tradition, has great weather, a low cost of living, and the friendliest people in the world. Of course, I knew all of this long before I decided to retire and move here, since I'd spent a good portion of my youth in San Antonio.

There was a small population boom in the early 1970s when massive building projects were underway in San Antonio to accommodate its swelling citizenry. A few blocks from my house on Bane Street, a huge plot of land was suddenly filled with several pieces of earth-moving equipment, whose operators went to work clearing the mesquite trees, flattening the landscape and carving places for streets. Several huge mounds of soil sprung up as if by magic, and my good friends Glen and Tommy and I had a new place to ride our bikes.

When not riding bicycles up and down these dirt monstrosities, we'd lie on their sloped banks and watch the activity going on around us. Except for the earliest part of the afternoon, when the sun was high in the sky, one side of these earthen structures was always shaded. That's the side where we'd hang out. When the shade moved, so did we, as we watched an endless beehive of construction work going on all around us. This is how we spent a good portion of the summer of 1971.

Of course, we spent a certain amount of time getting into mischief too. After the workers had gone home for the day, we'd climb aboard the huge Caterpillar earthmovers and road graders and pretend to drive them. A couple of them started without keys, and we'd start them up just to hear the engines roar. Looking back now, it's probably a very good thing we never put them into gear.

My friend Glen had taken auto shop in his junior year of high school that previous year, so he knew a lot more about cars and such than Tommy and I did. For example, he knew how to reach into a diesel engine's compartment and turn off the valve on the fuel line. He did this to several of the vehicles one evening , and we enjoyed the spectacle the following morning as the vehicle drivers scratched their heads, trying to figure out why none of their equipment wanted to start.

After the landscape was dotted with wooden stakes and bright orange pieces of surveyors tape, we spent the best part of a Sunday afternoon pulling up dozens of the stakes and moving them over a couple of feet. Current residents who may wonder why their neighbor's back yard is four feet wider (or narrower) than their own can probably blame us for that.

When the cement trucks started rolling in several at a time to start pouring the foundations for these houses, we made it our personal mission to write our initials in the corners of as many as possible. We'd simply wait until late evening, when the last of the workers left, and bounce from one slab to the next, leaving our marks. I'm sure those marks are still there today, in the corners of the living rooms of all those houses, although they're only seen occasionally when a carpet layer pulls up the old carpet to replace it with new.

Not long after the cement trucks finished, the lumber trucks started coming, dropping off huge bundles of lumber for the framers. About this same time, an old man in a blue Ford pickup truck began to drive through the area several times each evening. He told us his name was Juan, and he was there to protect the lumber from being pilfered.

Juan made a deal with us: he wouldn't mind us playing in the houses while they were under construction, if we'd help him keep an eye out for people who had a habit of driving their pickups into new developments at night and carting things away. We promised we'd write down the license number of any vehicle we saw involved in such activity, and Juan even gave us a notepad and pen for this purpose. As any grown man will attest, such a mission gives young boys a sense of purpose. We felt like private detectives, and from that point on made a real effort in helping Juan track the activity of anyone coming near our houses.

Of course, we never did see anyone actually stealing anything. I'd like to think it's because we did such a great job watching them. More likely, though, they just performed their thievery late at night, after we'd gone home and went to bed.

Toward the end of that summer, the project consisted of maybe thirty new homes on four newly paved streets, each in various stages of construction. When a team of framers finished erecting the walls of one house, they'd move down the street to perform the same process at another site. Another crew would pick up where they left off, adding plywood sheeting to the roof and exterior walls of the house they just finished.

There were several nights when, either too tired to ride our bikes, or caught up in the adventure of the moment, we chose to stay the night at the houses instead of going home. San Antonio is a temperate city, and its summer nights are comfortable enough for open-air camping with neither blankets nor fans. We made beds out of rolls of soft insulation material, with a plastic tarp thrown over the top. An occasional mosquito was the only thing that spoiled an otherwise good night's sleep.

One time during that particular summer, our friend Mike ran away from home, and we helped harbor him in the new development for several nights. Mike and his father just never saw things eye to eye, and Mike was sometimes the recipient of savage beatings. One night he came to Glen's front door when I was there and asked Glen if he could stay the night with him.

Mike's swollen face and blackened eyes told us immediately that this was serious, and we took him to one of the almost-finished houses at the far end of the construction site. During the several nights he was there, at least one of us spent each night with him to keep him company. Although Glen and Tommy's parents knew where Mike was, they did a good job of feigning ignorance when Mike's parents came looking for him. Glen's mom sent food and bottles of Coca-Cola for Mike a couple of times a day, and we made sure he always had someone to talk to.

I learned a lot about Mike's home life during those troubling few days, more than I really wanted to know, and I realized how lucky I was not to have been in the same situation. Eventually Mike went back home and things seemed to have calmed down a bit. Not long after that, Mike's mom took him and his little sister and moved away with them, and I never saw Mike again.

Sadly, our summer vacation came to an end, and so too did our visits to the construction site. We got involved in other things, like school and girls and other stuff, and simply stopped going.

Now that site is heavily developed with thirty year-old homes and tall trees. But in my memory it's still a group of brand new houses on bare ground and a small band of young boys enjoying a great adventure.

Getting Away From it All

There are certain milestones in every boy's life which he vividly remembers many years later. The first time he catches a fish without his father's help is one such event. The first time he kisses a girl, the first time he skips school and his first little league home run are others.

Perhaps not as common, but vividly remembered at least by this grown up boy, is one's first attempt at running away from home.

I said this might not be as common because I have learned over the years that many kids in my generation actually had good relationships with their parents. Or, at least as adults, most of my friends will never admit to running away from home as a kid.

Maybe it was just my neighborhood which, for whatever reason, had a higher percentage of kids who got mad at their parents. Whatever the case, virtually every boy I knew in my neighborhood in the 1960s ran away from home at least once. Maybe it was something in the water.

The vast majority of these excursions ended not long after dark. Generally, if a boy stormed out of the house in such a rage that he forgot to pack a sandwich, his resolve would last only until his stomach started growling. Once hungry, he would usually find it in his heart to forgive his parents for their transgressions, and he would return home.

Of course, in the cold winter months, there was another factor besides hunger that the runaway had to account for. Poor Wesley, who we nicknamed "the Brain," for a reason I can never remember, once ran away in the middle of December wearing a t-shirt and a pair of boxer shorts. No jacket, no pants, no shoes or socks, and obviously no working brain.

Wesley made it the few blocks to Mark's house in the middle of the night and knocked on Mark's bedroom window until Mark took pity on him and let him in, as he might a stray dog shivering at his back door and whimpering to come in. Wesley spent the rest of the night laying in Mark's spare bed, vowing never to go home again, and muttering about laying low until the next circus came to town, when he would join the traveling troup and leave Lubbock forever.

The next afternoon Wesley went sheepishly back home, dressed in Mark's clothes, and was dismayed to find that his parents hadn't even realized he was gone.

Weldon, who lived in the middle of the block one street up from us, was a frequent runaway. One day, Weldon's dad became enraged after discovering that Weldon had been pilfering condoms from his dad's dresser drawer to use as water balloons. His father removed his belt and proceeded to warm Weldon's backside with it. This was the custom in many of the neighborhood households back in the 1960s, including my own.

Weldon decided after it was all over that he would never again subject himself to such punishment. He said he was much too old for such an indignity. "After all," he said matter-of-factly, "I'm eleven years old, for cryin' out loud..."

Eleven year old Weldon packed some clothes into a paper grocery bag and spent the better part of the next two weeks bouncing around the neighborhood. Each night he'd stay with one of his friends, and each day he'd make arrangements for the next night's accommodations.

None of his friends' parents, of course, knew that Weldon hadn't seen or heard from his family in days. They simply knew that their son had invited a friend to stay for the night. By moving on each day, no parental suspicions were aroused, and Weldon had a warm place to sleep each night and hot meals to eat each day. He even got his laundry done occasionally when one of his friends would add his items to the family wash.

It was a classic battle of wills. Weldon's father told his older brother Carlton that he knew Weldon was staying with friends, and was therefore being taken care of. He vowed that he would not go looking for a "snot-nosed runaway kid."

Weldon, on the other hand, refused to go back to a family who didn't care enough to look for him, and wanted at least a nominal sign that they cared.

In the end, it was a problem of logistics that ended the standoff. Weldon simply ran out of places to stay. He'd already been to some of his friends' houses twice (those friends whose moms served good food), and he was afraid that by overdoing it he might raise suspicions. So he simply returned home one day, to his mother's great relief, Carlton's disdain (Carlton had started to like having his own room), and his father's indifference.

Weldon's mom then brokered a peace agreement that would have made Kissinger proud. Weldon would stay out of his father's dresser, and his father would never again whip him with a belt... at least for that particular transgression.

Of course, Weldon never ran out of other reasons for getting his hide tanned.

As for my own first attempt at running away, I was one of the wimps who decided that all was forgiven the first time my stomach told me it was time to eat. The only comment my mother made was "you're late for supper, where were you?"

A couple of hours earlier, before hunger overtook my anger, I likely would have responded with a smart-aleck retort. But not now, for I was starving and certainly didn't want to be sent to bed without supper.

"Uh... sorry. I was helping Larry fix his bike."

It was so good to be home again.

Payback

I've talked before about Mr. Damon Hill, my woodshop teacher the second time I attended ninth grade (that's another story for another time). This was at Slaton Junior High School in Lubbock, Texas in 1972.

I thought the world of Mr. Hill, as did every other kid in the class. He'd had a hard life, but had come through a winner, a champion for social justice, and was a genuinely nice guy. He was black and nearing 60, and I was a white teenager, and we had little in common other than a shared interest in woodworking. But he seemed to understand (to use a '70s term) "where I was coming from."

Slaton Junior High had its share of bullies, and did the other schools I attended when I was growing up. The worst of the bunch was Sandy Snead, who shared Mr. Hill's shop class with me and twenty or so other boys.

Sandy, for whatever reason, lacked any interest at all in woodshop, and tended to ease his boredom by antagonizing the rest of the class. Two days a week were instruction days, and the saws, lathes, and jointers were off limits on those days. On those days we had to sit quietly while Mr. Hill expanded our young minds with verbal instructions on the correct use of hand tools and woodworking techniques. Mr. Hill used to say that he hated those days as much as we did, because "you can't make furniture without getting your hands dirty." But verbal instruction was part of the curriculum, so he tolerated it as we did.

Each time Mr. Hill would turn his back or look away, Sandy Snead would thump the ear of the person sitting in front of him. Sandy had obviously been doing this for a considerable amount of time, for he was quite good at it, and it was quite painful to the unlucky recipient. Trouble was, Sandy was almost seven feet tall and outweighed most of the other students by fifty pounds of solid muscle. He therefore got away with his antics, as most of the boys would rather laugh off a sore ear than be beaten to a pulp in the school parking lot after school.

In a nutshell, Sandy was the typical "dumb jock" who used his size to push his way through life. It never occurred to him that maybe, just maybe, learning and developing some social skills might get him further than bullying others.

There was no assigned seating in Mr. Hill's shop class. The first boys to get there on any given day got their choice of seats. Those who beat Sandy to class got the seats in the back of the room so they wouldn't have to sit in front of him. Once Sandy arrived and took his seat, the desk in front of his instantly became the worst seat in the house, and the last one to be taken.

Unfortunately for me, I had science class fourth period, and shop class fifth period. That is significant because the science wing and the shop building were on opposite ends of the school. This meant that, even when I rushed through crowded hallways and skipped the traditional restroom and water fountain breaks, I was usually the last one to arrive at shop class.

About three months into the school year, I had grown weary of leaving woodshop with red, sore ears. I had hoped that Sandy would outgrow this juvenile behavior, but so far it hadn't happened, and it occurred to me that Sandy might behave as a ten-year old his entire life.

I visited Mr. Hill after school one day to pick up a lamp I'd made. I was going to take it home, and went through the process of polishing out the final coat of wax when Mr. Hill struck up a conversation.

"You know, if you wait too long to stand up to that boy, your ears are just going to fall off."

His comment caught me off guard. I believed, as Sandy had, that Sandy had been getting away with his antics, but Mr. Hill was obviously more observant than either of us thought.

I told Mr. Hill that I'd had my share of fistfights over the course of my youth, but that Sandy was different. He looked like a mountain to me, and would surely beat me into the ground if I fought back. Mr. Hill waved off my words by saying "Snead is a bully, and like all bullies, he's a coward at heart. He will keep doing what he's doing until someone shows him that it isn't acceptable behavior. Only then will he stop."

I guess I had assumed that because Mr. Hill and Sandy were both black, that he would automatically take Sandy's side. I was obviously wrong. I thought about it for a bit, and came to the conclusion that Mr. Hill was merely a man like any other, and that his skin color was irrelevant. Sandy, on the other hand, was just a punk, and Mr. Hill was right, somebody had to stand up to him. I just hoped that it wouldn't have to be me.

As the school year dragged on, I continued to draw the seat in front of Sandy, I continued to pay the price, and he continued to believe he was pulling the wool over the shop teacher's eyes.

Then one day things changed. I don't think I was in a particularly bad mood that day. I think I'd just finally had enough. I decided that if Sandy thumped my ear that day I was going to turn around and let him have it. I strode confidently into shop class that afternoon, sat directly in front of Sandy Snead, and waited with baited breath.

About ten minutes later I felt the sharp sting of Sandy's finger against my right ear. But I did nothing. For all my resolve, I was glued to my seat, absolutely paralyzed.

I sat and fumed, and the more I fumed, the madder I got. I was now madder at myself than I was at Sandy. I was furious with myself for once again letting him get away with inflicting pain at my expense.

A full five minutes had passed before I finally exploded. Without thinking, I sprang to my seat, turned around, and jumped into Sandy Snead with both fists. He'd obviously forgotten about thumping my ear and had refocused his attention to another area in the room, for the shocked look on his face told me that I caught him totally off guard. Or maybe he was just amazed that after all this time someone was finally standing up to him.

My first punch caught him solidly on the side of his chin. I followed up with a left jab that landed squarely on his nose, and another right that hit his left cheekbone, right below his temple. By this time he was cowering in his chair and trying his best to cover his face.

It ended as quickly as it started. I stood over him for a moment, then felt like a fool and sheepishly returned to my seat.

The room was silent for a few seconds before Sandy recovered enough to let loose a stream of profanity, while covering his nose and trying to stem the flow of bright red blood flowing from it. Curiously, his tirade was directed not at me, but at Mr. Hill. "Are you gonna let him do that to me, man?"

Mr. Hill calmly looked around the room and asked quietly to no one in particular "Did anyone see anything happen?" Dead silence. "Well, I didn't either," he said. "I guess I miss a lot that goes on in my class."

Sandy apparently got the message, and spent the rest of the class holding a shop towel against his nose and sulking. Mr. Hill asked me to stay after class, and I assumed he was going to take me to the vice principal's office for fighting. After the rest of the class cleared out, however, he said absolutely nothing, but offered a warm smile and a "high five."

I told him the next time he saw me would be at my funeral, since Sandy was sure to catch me after school and beat my brains out. "Nope, that won't happen," he said. "Bullies are just cowards. Once you show them you won't take any stuff off of them, they'll leave you alone."

I had my doubts, and looked over my shoulder all the way home that afternoon. But he was absolutely right. Sandy gave up thumping other peoples' ears, and the two of us even formed an uneasy friendship of sorts by school's end.

Although Mr. Hill and I came from vastly different backgrounds and from two different generations, I felt much closer to him from that day on. I felt we were somehow on the same team.

A Miserable Way to Die

I thought I was dying. My life had barely started, and now it was over. Here I was, a mere lad of ten years, lying on the cold tile floor of the boys' restroom on a warm spring afternoon, bleeding buckets of blood and feeling life slip slowly away.

It was April, 1969. On the campus of P.F. Brown Elementary School in Lubbock, Texas, my life was almost over. It was a fitting place to die, I suppose. Might as well end it where it began, and I was born just a few blocks from here. I was surrounded by my friends, so I wouldn't die alone, although it was true that my friends were only there because they were students and had to be. If they'd had a choice, they'd all be fishing instead.

Still, it could have been worse. I could have died on a snow covered hilltop, with no one around for miles to comfort me.

Not that my friends were much comfort. "C'mon, get up, ya big baby," cried Wesley, who had just stabbed me in the back with a yellow Number 2 pencil. "It can't hurt that bad! Get up before Mr. Autry comes in here!"

But I was paralyzed. I could feel the poison pouring from the pencil lead and creeping through my body, grabbing my nerves and turning them off, one by one, until it would finally reach my brain and I'd drift off into the great unknown. After all, we'd been briefed in health class about lead poisoning. They didn't warn of being stabbed in the back as a specific danger, but what greater lead poisoning hazard could there be, if not lead from a Number 2 pencil?

"Aw, its not so bad." Mark stated, matter-of-factly. Easy for him to say. He wasn't in the last throes of his life. "It's barely bleeding. Come on, get up, before the bell rings."

But the pain was unbearable. I couldn't move at all. I could barely breathe. And I swear I heard my heart stop beating. More than once.

Larry, ever helpful, told me to roll over on my side. But the agony was too great. So he rolled me over himself. Then he tenderly took hold of the pencil with the intention of gently pulling it out.

What happened next was the source of great debate for months. Larry said that I, being a big sissy and afraid of pain, jumped as he took hold of the pencil. I, on the other hand, maintained that a great and violent convulsion overtook my body and made me shake uncontrollably for a fraction of a second. As the song goes, that was my story and I was sticking with it.

Whatever version was the truth, the results were not debatable. The pencil lead broke off into my back and stayed there. Now I was doomed for sure.

My so-called friends looked in disbelief at the pencil in Larry's hand. From the way I'd been yelling, they thought the pencil had been imbedded in my back three or four inches. Now they saw that it was embedded only a quarter of an inch. There wasn't even any blood on the pencil. They made it a point to wave the pencil in front of my face to drive that point home.

Now, I don't know what happened to all that missing blood. I just knew that despite the evidence to the contrary, I was indeed dying. I knew because I could feel the blood pouring out of the large gaping hole in my back where the pencil had been. I knew that by this time I had lost a couple hundred gallons of blood, at least.

They say that in a crisis, seconds seem like hours, and minutes like days. That was true that fateful day when Wesley playfully stabbed me in the back with a pencil. For it seemed like an eternity as I lay painfully bleeding on that bathroom floor, as my friends tried their best to coerce me to get up and go back to class.

Then, in my delirium, I looked up to find my friends gone. I was all alone.

Perhaps I had died and gone to heaven (I was quite the optimist in those days). That was it, of course. That would explain why none of my friends were still there. Then it dawned on me that heaven looked an awful lot like the elementary school's restroom.

Then the tardy bell rang, and I realized that my friends had deserted me, leaving me to die my horrible death alone just so they could make it back to class on time. Disgusted and angry, I painfully stumbled to my feet and dragged my weakened and mutilated body down the hall to the nurse's office.

"Why aren't you in class?"

With my last breath I told her I was stabbed in the back with a lead pencil, then abandoned to die by my friends. She told me to take off my shirt and examined the wound.

I expected a shocked gasp, some sympathy, and immediate first aid. Instead, I got a nonchalant "You'll be okay."

I was dumbfounded. This so-called angel of mercy told me there was no blood, that the pencil had barely broken the skin, and that I should stop sniveling and go back to class.

"But the lead broke off. I'll die of lead poisoning." I protested.

"It's not really lead, its graphite," she countered without missing a beat. "It'll probably eventually dissolve. Even if it doesn't, your skin will grow over it and you'll be fine."

Disgusted with the diagnosis, but nonetheless happy to be alive, I stumbled back to class. Wesley eventually apologized, and we went on to other things. I'd forgotten about it completely, until one day years later, when one of my high school buddies asked me if the pencil lead was still in my back. After doing a considerable search of our collective memories, we finally remembered the general vicinity where I'd suffered my near-mortal wound. We checked, and there was no sign that the lead was still there. I guess I cheated death.

Now, all I have to worry about is reading a newspaper some day when I'm old and gray, and coming across an article about the perils of graphite poisoning.

By the way, if the Number 2 pencil is the most popular pencil in the world, how come it's still number 2? Food for thought...

Freshman Blues

The transition from middle school to high school is a monumental step for a kid. In the last year of middle school, a boy is a big man on campus, at the top of the mountain. He has survived three years of hideous teachers, grueling work, and unreasonable demands on his time. Younger kids look up to him, call him "your highness," and step aside when he walks down the hallway. He has arrived. At least temporarily.

Next school year, this walking success story slips and rolls down that mountain, and will pick himself up bruised and bloodied, to find that he has become the lowest life form on earth: a freshman.

A freshman is hated by everyone, from the teachers who go out of their way to make life a living hell, to the high school janitors who empty the lunchroom garbage into freshmens' lockers late at night.

Everyone thinks it's a world of fun to play pranks on freshmen. After all, they are barely more than single-cell organisms; wild-eyed geeks who expect to be abused and tend to accept their fate without much complaint.

Should a freshman attempt to fight back just once, he is kidnapped from class by all the senior players on the football team and tied to the tackling dummy. To add insult to injury the coach, instead of rescuing the poor kid, tells him "Hey, you're just a freshman; you're supposed to feel pain. Try not to bleed on my field, or I'll make you clean it up."

The same thing happens to a freshman who takes his case to that evil maintainer of discipline in high school, the vice principal. "Quit whining," the devil's spawn might say with a hideous smirk. "You have detention hall for the next five weeks. Now go back to the football field and clean up that blood!"

Actually, starting high school wasn't that bad for me, but my freshmen and I did have to accept a certain amount of abuse. Most of us were suckered into buying an elevator pass on the first day of school, for a school that had no elevator. I also bought a pass to the teachers' lounge, which I was told entitled me to pop in between classes and chill with the faculty in their own environment. At least I didn't buy two elevator passes, like my buddy Wesley did. He never did explain how he was going to ride two elevators at the same time.

We all did the initiation rites, like pushing a penny down the stairs with our noses, and we each had to pull off a prank of some kind. Mine was to plant a delayed smoke bomb in the hallway during one of the passing periods between classes.

The delay mechanism was a brilliant device that could only have been invented by a kid. A standard smoke bomb and a cigarette pilfered from one of the hoods behind the school combined to make a smoky weapon that would go off about five minutes after it was lit.

I took the cigarette and poked a hole all the way through it, just above the filter. Then, after inserting the smoke bomb's fuse through the hole, I lit the cigarette and gently placed it under one of the old radiators in the main hallway. Then I shuffled nonchalantly back to class.

Right on schedule, five minutes later, the cigarette burned down far enough to ignite the fuse, the smoke bomb went off, and all the students at Lubbock High School evacuated the building to take a twenty minute break from learning.

The nice thing about freshman pranks was that after you'd officially completed your assigned prank, you were considered (almost) one of the group. You had passed through the portal of acceptance and were now recognized as a card-carrying, contributing member of high school society. Although you were still technically a lowly freshman, you were no longer looked at with disgust. It was only at that point that you could finally breathe a sigh of relief, and be reasonably confident that you would no longer be killed for the pleasure of sadistic seniors.

By the end of the day, the rest of the school knows you. You might even get a smile from one of the junior cheerleaders and a thumbs up from a couple of the guys on the football team.

And, hey, it could have been worse. Wesley had to sneak into the basketball team's locker room and fill the coach's shampoo bottle with Nair.

My youngest daughter, Stephanie, somehow managed to survive her freshman year last year. Now that she's a sophomore, she thinks she's one tough turkey.

I'm just relieved because I no longer have to worry about her quite so much. The rest of her high school career should be a piece of cake.

The Fortune Teller

For many years an old house stood next to the old Preston Milk Store on 34th Street, not far from my house. It was a small frame residential home in the middle of a long stretch of street zoned for commercial businesses.

Presumably, it had been there longer than the zoning laws which allowed businesses on the street, and was left behind as, one by one, neighboring houses were torn down and commercial buildings were built in their places. That would explain why that old house looked like it was a million years old to me.

Except for its age, the only other thing distinctive about this house was the large sign out in front. "FORTUNES TOLD," it said in large purple letters on a canary yellow background. "Palms Read" appeared in slightly smaller green letters directly below. It was probably the ugliest sign ever erected anywhere.

Now, I have nothing against fortune tellers or palm readers in general. Just this one. For this was the one who stiffed me for three dollars.

Earning pocket money is sometimes pretty tough for a kid who doesn't get any allowance. If you're too young to get a job at a fast food restaurant, you're pretty much at the mercy of the occasional odd jobs that come along.

For Kent and I, a good portion of our spring and summer each year was spent doing yard work for strangers.

This wasn't the $75 mowing jobs that you and I contract out for today, paying adults with fancy pickup trucks and riding lawnmowers. Our service was much more personal.

We offered a good deal: we mowed the entire lawn, always swept up the sidewalks, and picked up any litter we found laying around, preferably before the lawnmower ate it. (It was much easier that way). For our efforts we charged one rate for everybody: three dollars. A fair price for a good product.

Life's Lessons From A Candy Machine

The day I went to the fortune teller's house, I was working alone. Kent was off with his family visiting his grandparents. I wasn't happy about doing all the work myself, but the prospect of keeping all the money definitely appealed to me. Anyway, the fortune teller was about seventy years old, with gray hair tied up in a tight bun. She seemed absolutely ancient to me at the time. She offered a toothless grin when she opened the door.

"You want your fortune told, young man?" she asked.
"Uh, no, ma'am, I wanted to see if you wanted your yard mowed."

She looked past me to the lawn, which was unkempt and full of weeds. It seemed to dawn on her that maybe a manicure for her lawn might be good for business. "How much?" she asked.

"Three dollars." I told her. She winced just a bit, then paused before saying with a flourish and wave of her hand, "Very well. Go ahead."

I remember struggling through the tall grass, half sorry that Kent wasn't there to relieve me occasionally, and half glad that he wasn't. Since I was on my own, I could afford to step next door after the job was done and get a large cherry Icee at the Preston Milk Store. I could enjoy it at my leisure, and then walk away with my usual cut of $1.50 plus some left over.

The thought of that Icee kept me going for the two hours it took me to finish mowing.

At last! I finished sweeping up just as rush hour traffic started driving down 34th Street. Although I had no watch, I knew this was a sign that supper would be ready soon and I needed to start heading home. I put my broom onto the lawnmower, wedging it between the motor and the handle so it wouldn't fall off. Then I went back to the fortune teller's door to get paid.

Several knocks... no answer. Several more... same result.

I knew she was still home. There were no cars that came or went while I was there. I knocked louder. Still no answer. I began to get an uneasy feeling in the pit of my stomach.

About that time, a car pulled into the driveway. A customer. I stepped back as a lady about thirty, in a brightly flowered dress, stepped onto the porch and tapped lightly on the door.

The door opened. The fortune teller stepped away from the door so the lady could enter, cast me a wicked glance, and told me "come back later." I knew then that I'd been had.

Crestfallen, I stumbled home. No Icee. No pocket money. Just a valuable lesson about human nature.

Although I visited the house several times over the next few weeks, I never got a response, other than an occasional flutter of the window curtains that told me she knew I was there.

The old house was torn down several years ago. All that remains of it now rests in the deep recesses of my memory. The fortune teller, judging from her advanced age when I met her, certainly went to meet her maker long ago. If I ever have a chance to meet her again, perhaps in a better place, I have something to say to her:

"You still owe me three bucks, lady."

Leadership in a Box

Spring, 1966: I very distinctly remember poring over the ad in the Boys' Life magazine. It was for a company with a name like "Leadership Sales Club," or "American Leadership Club," or something along those lines. The message to me was clear. If I sent in this postage-paid card, I would become a leader! Not only that, but I could win great prizes or cash too!

Visions of grandeur danced through my head. No telling what this might lead to. President of the United States? Maybe something even better: one of the Mercury astronauts? With membership in a leadership club, there would be no boundaries to where I would go or what I would accomplish.

All I had to do was mail the card. And since no postage was required, I wouldn't even have to explain to Mom or Dad why I needed a stamp. Terrific!

Six weeks later, just as advertised, a rather large box came in the mail. It was full of greeting cards. All I had to do to be a leader was to sell the cards, send in the money, and get some free prizes. Sounded simple enough.

The box also included a sales kit, with instructions on how to become a successful salesman, which obviously was a prerequisite to being a leader. Greet the potential customer with a kind word, the instructions said. Look them directly in the eye. Show them the samples included in the kit, and remind them that everyone has friends and relatives who need an occasional birthday greeting or a card at Easter or Christmas. What a piece of cake this was gonna be.

I suckered my kid brother Randy into the business. That is to say, I offered him the chance to become a leader as well. I did this because I wanted to give him the same opportunities I was to have in becoming a world diplomat, an airline pilot, or doctor. Plus, I needed a wagon. He had one, and I didn't.

We started out on a hot summer morning with everything we needed. The wagon was full of cards, samples, sales instructions, order forms for additional cards, and our lunch.

We had the foresight to know that our success would be of such a magnitude that it would prevent us from being able to take a lunch hour. So we'd have to eat on the run. But hey, that's what successful executives – successful leaders – have to do sometimes.

Our first potential customer was a gray haired lady in her late 60s, who looked a lot like my grandmother. This was a very good sign, because everyone knows that grandmothers will buy anything. All you have to do is go into any grandmother's house anywhere and look at all the worthless stuff lying around. This would definitely be an easy first sale.

I greeted her with a kind word: "It's so nice to see you today..." I looked her directly in her wrinkled old eye. I showed her the samples that came with my leadership kit. I reminded her that she had relatives and friends who needed an occasional birthday greeting or Christmas card. I got her door closed in my face.

Okay, so the first sale didn't happen. She must have been in a bad mood. Maybe one of her cats left a dead mouse on her pillow or something. No matter. A leader cannot get discouraged when he suffers an occasional setback. On to the next house.

Randy and I saw a lot of different doors that day. Many didn't open at all, although we could often hear voices or television sets on the other side of them. Many people were polite, and explained that it was only June, and they'd rather wait until Christmas to buy Christmas cards. Logic I couldn't really argue with.

Some simply didn't recognize our leadership potential and were downright rude, telling us to get lost or slamming their doors in our faces.

At the end of a long hot day, we'd sold a total of three boxes of cards. Two were to Randy's grade school teacher the previous school year, who didn't really need any cards, but bought them anyway because he was "such a joy to have in class."

Downtrodden and exhausted, we stumbled back home. Our samples had turned to mush from our sweaty palms, and from being passed too many times from hand to hand. Our lunch, half-eaten, was just too unappetizing to finish. The wagon, although a tiny bit lighter, seemed to weigh many times more than the one we started out pulling several hours earlier.

We learned several things that summer. We learned that you cannot package leadership in a box and mail it to someone. We learned that selling greeting cards door to door is just plain hard work. We learned that sales claims, like numerous other things we would encounter later in life, were not true simply because they were printed on paper. And we decided that neither of us ever, ever, wanted to sell anything again. Not ever.

Most of all, we learned that parents will help you out in a pinch. Ours didn't have to buy cards again for years. And I never did become a Mercury astronaut, something I still blame on the American Leadership Sales Company, or whatever it was called.

The Day I Didn't Meet Mickey Mantle

It was to be a great adventure, something we'd pass on to our grandchildren, a memory to stay with us the rest of our lives. Since I'm writing about it, I guess that part of it came about. But most of what happened on the day we set out to meet Mickey Mantle definitely didn't go according to plan.

We first heard of his coming on a Wednesday afternoon. Wesley was with his dad when they ran into Walter Bowling at the grocery store. Mr. Bowling was one of the teachers at our elementary school, and he asked Wesley's father in passing whether he was taking Wesley to see Mickey Mantle when he came to town.

The hero of the New York Yankees was to be at the grand opening of a Mickey Mantle Restaurant across town the following Saturday afternoon. Wesley's dad said no, he had no plans to take him. But that was okay, because we had our own plans.

This was to be the farthest any of us had ever traveled by bicycle. Because of the distance involved, and the travel time, it would be an all-day affair. Our plan was to sneak out early in the morning in time to be there to meet "Mick" at his 1 p.m. arrival time. Then we'd get his autograph, hang out with him at the restaurant for most of the afternoon, and set out in time to make it home before dark. It was a good plan… what could possibly go wrong?

It was hard to concentrate on anything else that Friday afternoon in school. Most of our time was spent passing notes back and forth across the back of the classroom. "What if they're not really passing out free food?" "No problem. We'll pack sandwiches and buy a pop to drink." "What if we have a flat?" "Larry just bought a patch kit. I'll bring a wrench." And so it went, until by the end of the school day we'd had most of the plan worked out. After school we just fine-tuned it.

We'd covered even the finest details. Wesley lived the farthest away, so he'd set out first. When he got to our houses, he'd tap on our windows to wake us up; then he'd rest while we were getting dressed. We'd all make sandwiches the night before and hide them in our bedrooms. By the time everyone else in our houses got up, we'd be long gone.

The first thing to go wrong was the "good night's sleep" we all needed to make the long bike ride. Although none of us were really fans of the Yankees, we all knew and liked Mickey Mantle. The prospect of meeting him and shaking his hand was just too much excitement. We all spent half the night staring at our ceilings before finally drifting off to sleep from sheer exhaustion.

Then Wesley overslept. Luckily, Larry thought to set his alarm clock, so he got the rest of us up in time. Still, we had to wait for Wesley, so his blunder put us considerably behind schedule.

Next, Kent arrived to explain that his cat found the liver cheese sandwiches he had hidden under his bed, and had a good time feasting on them. Worse, his mom was in the kitchen having coffee, so he couldn't sneak in to make more.

Ronnie fell while climbing out his window and hurt his knee. He arrived steering his bike with one hand and carrying his sandwiches with the other. "How in heck are we supposed to carry these dumb sandwiches?" he said as he rode up.

We all looked at each other. No one thought to ask that particular question before. Back then, the backpacks and book bags that kids carry today simply didn't exist. Neither did plastic grocery bags. If they did, we could have just put the sandwiches into a bag and carried it onto our back or tied it to our handle bars. But we didn't have that option. Wesley, normally the genius in our group, was still nowhere in sight.

Larry finally came up with a solution: "Let's tape them to the sissy bars." Sissy bars were long bars that attached the back of our "banana seats" to our bikes, and rose high over our heads, allowing us to lean back and relax as we rode. And, no, I don't know why they called them "sissy bars."

It was crude method of transport, but it seemed like a reasonable option, and the sandwiches didn't raise any concerns.

We were almost an hour behind schedule by the time Wesley finally showed up. At least we didn't have to worry about taping down his lunch; he forgot it.

We tested our stamina that morning, peddling furiously instead of at the leisurely pace we had planned, in order to get to the restaurant before 1 p.m. None of us had a watch, so we believed Wesley when he swore that he could tell the time by looking at the sun. He assured us that we had plenty of time to spare.

It was easy to tell when we were getting close, because we could see the crowd from two blocks away.

We had no idea that Mickey Mantle was so popular in Texas. We began to doubt that we'd even get to see him, much less shake his hand and hang out with him.

We mingled with the crowd, waiting patiently and looking around for the free food that we had heard (and were hoping beyond hope) would be there. No food. Worse, we quickly found out: no Mickey Mantle either.

We never did find out why Mickey Mantle didn't wait for us to arrive. In our young minds, he just couldn't or wouldn't have left before we got there. But he did. Never mind the fact that he didn't know us, or know that we were trying desperately to get there in time. Thinking rationally is not something adolescent boys often do in situations such as this.

Perhaps he had a perfectly good reason. Perhaps he had to get to practice. Maybe he was had to visit a sick kid. It didn't really matter. From that point on, the Mickey Mantle fiasco served to severely tarnish the image of one of America's premier baseball heroes, at least in the minds of five young boys from Lubbock, Texas.

We stumbled home that evening exhausted, hungry, and wishing Mickey Mantle would strike out every at-bat for the rest of his career. Still, the trip was an adventure, and still serves up pleasant memories even forty years later.

Lunch time!

To a young boy in grade school on a warm spring day, nothing is worse than having to sit in a classroom, looking out the window, watching the clouds roll by. I remember the skies being much bluer then, and smelling so much cleaner. The clouds were whiter and fluffier and held more interesting shapes. The clouds of today are boring. I've tried with my children and grandchildren to find characters or things in the clouds, like I used to do when I was young. Apparently I've lost that ability. Today a cloud to me is, well, just a cloud...

Anyway, that's the kind of daydreaming a young boy does as he sits in class on a beautiful day, letting his mind wander, much more concerned about the world outside than on academia. That's why it was so important that we broke from the physical bounds of the schoolyard every chance we got.

Lunch time! Even today, I suspect, this time in the middle of the school day holds a special place in the hearts of youngsters everywhere. It was especially so for me in the sixth grade, as this was our chance to leave P.F.Brown Elementary School for forty precious minutes. Forty minutes, all to ourselves. No teachers, no books, nothing but time. Somehow the air smelled sweeter off the school grounds. This must have been what freedom smelled like.

Forty minutes in adult time doesn't seem like an awful lot. But a small group of boys with energy to burn can get an awful lot accomplished in forty minutes. Or get into an awful lot of mischief. Which option we took generally depended on how much change we had in our pockets.

Our lunchtime escapades would invariably start with a quick headcount, just to make sure we had everybody.

"Where's Jody?"

"Aw, he was being a baby," his brother Ronnie might offer, "Mom let him stay home today..."

The resulting disappointed whines were in no way to be interpreted as sympathy for a sick playmate, nor sorrow for the loss of his company. They were rooted in the fact that we now had a problem pooling enough money for pizza.

"Let's see, we have $2.17," Wesley might say as he counted our meager contributions of lunch money and all the spare pennies and nickels we could muster from the depths of our pockets. "That'll be enough, if we split a coke." Back then we thought of Wesley as the brains of the group, although I knew him through high school and my assessment of his intellect eventually dropped considerably.

Off to the pizza parlor. First, an all-out sprint to the 34th Street strip mall three streets away. Past the U.V. Blake record store, where we'd be hanging out listening to records if we hadn't had enough money to buy pizza. Past the Party Hut, which we loved for the "neat" practical jokes they sold. Past Lubbock Drug Store, with its old fashioned soda counter and grumpy proprietor, who had a nasty habit of tossing us out occasionally for being too rowdy. Past the bakery with its tasty donuts, and finally, to the holy grail of lunchtime establishments, Plains Pizza.

In 1964 a cheese pizza cost $1.55 plus tax. It wasn't a large pizza by any means. It certainly wasn't enough to fill the empty stomachs of four hungry boys. But it was delightful. I remember it being so much better than the fast food pizza of today. Homemade sauce seasoned perfectly without the aid of preservatives or artificial flavor, fresh enough to contain an occasional piece of tomato that still tasted like a piece of tomato. Real mozzarella cheese coarsely grated, delicious crust crunchy on the outside, yet soft and piping hot on the inside. Whatever happened to pizza like that?

By the time our pizza came we never had more than five minutes to eat it. Not a problem for us, since we were used to eating on the run when we had to. Now, of course, we were happy that Jody wasn't able to join us, since one less lunch mate meant bigger portions for the rest of us.

By far the best thing about lunch at Plains Pizza wasn't the pizza, though, it was Angela. Angela was a dark-haired beauty who attended school at nearby Texas Tech College, as it was called back then. Angela was an object of our affection not only because she was young and pretty and flirted with us, but also because she always managed to get our pizza out just in time for us to wolf it down, regardless of how heavy the lunchtime crowd was. A very belated thanks to you, Angela, wherever you are.

Anyway, once the pizza was gone, it was another quick sprint back to the school, albeit at a slightly slower pace now that our bellies were full. Then we'd wait outside the school for the bell to ring so we could return to class, stopping at the water fountain to quench our thirsts and make up for having to share a drink at the pizza place (darn that Jody, anyhow). Then it would be back to the classroom, to spend the rest of the afternoon belching from the rich pizza sauce, grossing out the girls, staring out the window, and seeing Angela's face in the clouds. I've wondered many times over the years what became of Angela...

The Prairie Dog Fiasco

For millions of years, long before man inhabited the wind-swept plains and canyons of west Texas, a nondescript little creature called the "prairie dog" called this country home.

Actually, "nondescript" doesn't do an adequate job of describing this animal. Perhaps "ugly" would be a better word. And despite his name, he looks absolutely nothing like a dog. He is a large rodent, perhaps twice the size of a guinea pig, with a stiff yellow fur and a penchant for digging. Prairie dogs live below ground, digging colonies like ants, and their intricate burrows interconnect into a series of tunnels which allow them a life safe from predators like hawks and real dogs.

Perhaps the prairie dog got his name from his habit of yelping, in dog-like fashion, when startled.

Anyway, these creatures roamed freely across the countryside where I grew up. Since they were a rather shy lot, they tended to steer clear of developed areas, and my friends and I lived in the middle of the city. So one day when my pal Wesley decided he wanted to catch a prairie dog and train him as a pet, we knew we had an adventure on our hands.

First, we tried to talk Wesley out of it. Although we knew where a large colony of prairie dogs lived, it was quite a bike ride, and these were the dog days of summer. It was much easier sitting under a shade tree chewing on a blade of grass and talking about the meaning of life, than peddling our Schwinns six miles in one hundred degree heat.

We came up with a dozen good reasons why we shouldn't go. Ronnie's tire kept going flat, we said, and our parents wouldn't let us go that far. Further, how would we catch the little monster, and how would we get him home?

For every logistical problem we came up with, though, we grew more and more excited about the prospect of catching a prairie dog and delivering him to Wesley's house.

By the time we finished talking Wesley out of the idea, we had talked ourselves into it.

This would be our farthest bicycle trip that summer. The previous year, we had wasted a trip across town in a vain attempt to see Mickey Mantle, and had returned home exhausted, vowing never to ride our bikes that far again. But this was different. This time, we knew where the prairie dogs lived. Since they weren't rich spoiled ballplayers, we wouldn't have to worry about them ruining our fun by not being there. Even better, we'd get to bring a prairie dog home with us and make a pet out of him. We couldn't have done that with Mickey Mantle.

Our plan was simple. When we packed our lunches for the trip, we'd pack an extra peanut butter and jelly sandwich to use as bait. We'd flatten out a small box, and Wesley would strap the box to his back on the trip. Once at the colony, we'd reassemble the box, catch the rodent, and take turns carrying the box back to Wesley's house.

In our underdeveloped brains, fueled perhaps by a bit of testosterone, was a macho need to make this happen, to prove to ourselves and others that we were worthy hunters. We thought it would be a piece of cake.

But there was immediate dissension in the ranks. "Why do I have to carry the box?" Wesley complained in his typically whiny, high-pitched voice.

"Because, ya big dummy," Mark explained as he rolled his eyes, "you're keeping the prize, you should at least carry the box. Besides, the hard part will be carrying the box back, and we'll take turns doing that." Not even Wesley could find the fault in that logic.

And so it was that we set off on our latest adventure early that Saturday morning. Mark had confiscated a couple of one quart Cragmont creme soda bottles that his mom had planned to take back to the local Safeway for her nickel deposit refund. He had rinsed them out, filled them with water, and placed them into a cloth laundry bag. Back then, backpacks simply didn't exist. So we all threw our sandwiches into the laundry bag with the water bottles and took turns carrying it over our shoulders on the long ride to the prairie dog colony.

Halfway to our destination, we stopped for lunch, to find that the heavy bottles of water had crushed our sandwiches into mush. No matter. They still tasted the same, and we were hungry enough not to care. We were thirsty enough, as we passed the water around, not to care about the tiny pieces of white bread floating in the water, placed there inadvertently by those drinking before us. Heck, we were boys, after all. The same ones who pricked our fingers several years before and mixed our blood, becoming "blood brothers" for all eternity. A few "floaties" in our water weren't going to hurt us.

Refreshed and rejuvenated, we remounted our trusty steeds and set out again for the outskirts of town where the prairie dogs lived. Once there, we reassembled the flattened box and set it up not far from one of the colony's entrances. We'd seen a fat prairie dog disappear down that particular hole as we rode up on our bikes, and figured that was a good spot to set our trap.

Directly under the box, we placed the sad, deformed mess of smeared purple and brown sweetness that was once a peanut butter and jelly sandwich. The sun was now high in the sky, and we figured that if the bait didn't attract one of these ugly little animals, perhaps the shade under the box would.

We found a stick and used it to prop up one end of the box. Our plan was to stay back until the prairie dog came out of the hole, and let him eat the sandwich until he accidentally knocked the stick out from under the box. We hoped that he'd be so busy eating that he wouldn't notice the box falling over him until he was trapped beneath it. Then we'd race to the box and pounce on it before he had a chance to get out of it.

Of course, our schemes rarely went according to plan, and this one was no exception. First, the wind kept blowing the box over. Then the prairie dogs, too timid to come out, or perhaps catching our scent, refused to budge. Finally, after two frustrating hours, a mangy little prairie dog stuck his head out of the hole and sniffed the air.

We grew more and more apprehensive as the rodent inched his way out of the burrow and toward the box. It was obvious that the smell of the sandwich had piqued his curiosity.

After several minutes, the suspicious creature worked his way to the box, crouched underneath it, and began pushing the sandwich around with his nose. Then his tiny tail caught the stick and sent it tumbling, and the box came down just as planned to capture him inside.

For a second, everyone froze. We were shocked, I think, that our plan had actually worked. The prairie dog, perhaps lulled by the darkness into thinking he was hidden, didn't move either. Or perhaps he was just too busy chewing on the sandwich to care. Whatever the case, we all made it to the box and held it down, so that our prize had no chance of getting out.

It was only then that we saw the fatal flaw in our insidious plan. "How in heck do we close the box?" Ronnie asked.

It was a fair question. We had failed to plan that far ahead. The flaps that we'd need to close the box were folded up inside of it. If we lifted up the box to fold down the flaps, the prairie dog would run away. We felt like a bunch of idiots, and rightfully so.

We tried lifting the edge of the box very slightly while Mark slipped his hand inside. A split second later there was a quick rustle of activity inside the box and a lot of flying dust. Mark quickly retracted his hand and cursed at the "stupid mutt" for biting his finger.

We sat for another half hour, looking pitifully at that box, and trying to find a way to turn it over and seal it without our prize getting out. We were mad at ourselves for being so stupid, getting hungry again, and beginning to lose our patience. Not even Wesley, who was well known in our circle for being able to think on his feet, could come up with a solution.

Eventually, we admitted that we'd lost. Wesley was heartbroken that he wasn't going to have the coolest pet in the neighborhood, so the least we could do was let him have the honor of setting the little fellow free.

Wesley slowly lifted the box, and we all expected the prairie dog to take off like a rocket. Mark wanted to kick him to pay him back for the bite on his finger, but he knew we'd all pulverize him if he did. So he just stood back and sulked.

Oddly enough, when the box came off, the rodent just sat there for several seconds. Perhaps he was gloating because he'd won this battle of wills against this allegedly superior bunch of humans. Maybe he was just adjusting his eyes to the bright sunlight. Or maybe he was waiting to see if we were going to give him another sandwich. Whatever it was, it ended after a few seconds when he took off like a shot and disappeared down a nearby hole.

It was a long trip home. About the only good thing about it was we didn't have to argue about whose turn it was to carry the box.

By the time we got back to Wesley's house, we were tired, dirty, and starving.

For a long time after that trip, nobody talked about it. I think we were still licking our wounds, for our pride was hurt. But looking back, it wasn't a bad way to spend a day.
To see prairie dogs in Lubbock these days, you have to go to the local state park. There sits a walled sanctuary where a couple hundred of the critters now live, fed whole peanuts and bread crumbs by visitors who gather there by the dozens to take photos. I read somewhere that prairie dogs live to be 50 years old or more. I wonder if there's a withered old resident of that sanctuary who still laughs at us occasionally, and wonders when we're going to bring him another peanut butter and jelly sandwich.

The Dance

They say that music soothes the savage beast, and it may well be true. I saw on the news the other day that some of the street gangs in Los Angeles are putting aside their weapons and their differences and attending dances together in neutral territories, both to raise legitimate funds and to improve community relations. Apparently, to the surprise of many, the idea is working. Rival gangs are apparently enjoying themselves, enjoying each others' company, and leaving under better terms.

I am reminded of the first, and last, dance I attended with Shirley Ann Gandera when we were teenagers in San Antonio so many years ago. Back then, the problems with gang wars and disputed turf wasn't yet a major problem. But racial relations often were.

Shirley Ann was Hispanic, a brown-skinned beauty with raven-colored hair and deep brown eyes that made me melt when I gazed into them. She was everything I wanted and needed in a girlfriend, and I fell head over heels in love with her. It didn't matter to either of us that I, being white, had little in common with her family and friends. It also didn't matter that some of her siblings, and many of her neighbors, weren't particularly pleased when I came to visit.

It wasn't just one-sided. I recall one time when my good friend Glen and I came to blows because he made a crude remark about Shirley Ann. He quickly apologized, and we put it past us, but it served to show both of us the ugly side of racism and prejudice, even from those who claim to be racially tolerant.

Shirley Ann invited me to a dance one Saturday night at a community center in our neighborhood in south San Antonio. The band was to be Chicano, the music Tejano, sung mostly in Spanish that I could not understand. What's more, she said, there might be some people who would take offense to my being there.

It didn't matter. The fact was that Shirley Ann wanted me to be there, and I could think of no place in the entire world I'd rather be on that particular Saturday night.

We arrived at about 8 p.m., long after the dance had started. By the time we walked in the door, it was pretty much in full swing. Everyone was laughing, dancing, and having a good time. Although the patrons of this dance were mostly teenagers, there were plenty of quart bottles of Budweiser beer being passed around for all to indulge in. It seemed as though everyone was having a blast.

We didn't cause too much of a stir initially. A few heads turned, and a few people whispered into each others' ears. But no one blocked my way, and the majority of the group smiled warmly and said "hola," as we made our way to the dance floor.

Being teenagers, most of us were mediocre dancers at best. The boys had generally mastered one particular style of dance. Swaying from side to side, we'd rock our upper bodies and move our arms to the beat of the music. There were a couple of good dancers in the crowd, but the floor was too crowded for them to show off their moves. My initial fear that my lack of dancing talent would be obvious to all quickly left me, as I saw that I fit right in with almost everyone else.

But my skin was still lighter than everyone else's. This first became a problem when one of Shirley Ann's friends challenged her when we came off the dance floor for a break. "Why couldn't you bring Julio or Robert," she demanded to know, "instead of him?" When she referred to me, she cast an evil look in my direction, and the tone of her voice was acidic.

"His name is Darrell, and he's here because he's the one I wanted to be with." Shirley Ann never lost her composure, or her cool. When her friend began speaking in Spanish, Shirley Ann continued to respond in English, out of obvious consideration for me. Her friend finally gave up, spouted a couple of obscenities, and stormed off.

I came fully prepared, and even expected, to be involved in a fist fight. I thought it would be that ugly. But the rest of the evening went relatively smoothly. It might have been the illegal alcohol that encouraged everyone to lose their prejudices as well as their inhibitions. It may, as I alluded to earlier, have been the music that kept tempers from flaring. Or maybe it was because most of the crowd knew and liked Shirley Ann. Maybe they decided that her choice of a dancing partner was her business alone, and they had no right to question it.

Maybe it was a combination of the three. Whatever it was, Shirley Ann and I thoroughly enjoyed the evening. For me, it was one of the highlights of our relationship. By the time we walked out of the dance hall that night, I felt considerably more at ease, and maybe a little more accepted by this group of people.

This opened several doors for me personally, and made it easier for Shirley Ann and I spend time together. At school, brown faces which had glared at me in the past now offered friendly smiles and warm greetings. Although I could never be a real part of their culture, I was at least accepted by the Hispanic crowd, many of whom referred to me merely as "Shirley Ann's boyfriend."

I didn't mind the title. And the experience was invaluable. It showed me that we are all alike in most ways. Prejudice is born not of reason but of ignorance and fear. As Rodney King once put it, "Can't we all just get along?"

The answer to that question is yes, we can. It just takes a little effort. If the street gangs of Los Angeles have indeed found a way of ridding the streets of violence by replacing it with music, then I wish them the best of luck. It's a shame we didn't try this many lost lives ago.

Mercado Lopez

America was built by the small entrepreneur, who was willing to risk his worldly possessions in an effort to build upon them. That spirit is still alive, and is one of the wheels which keep America rolling along. Sometimes, if local laws and zoning requirements get in the way of these folks, the rules are bent, twisted, or outright broken, depending on the need.

I lived in San Antonio, Texas, for a few years while I was growing up. My neighborhood was on the low end of middle class, a gathering of humble homes that were comfortable, and which provided the essentials of life, but apparently weren't the type which gave off signals to developers that here was a neighborhood with a lot of money to spend.

For that reason, our neighborhood didn't have the usual convenience store at each end of the block. The nearest convenience store to my house was almost a mile away.

This definitely took the convenience out of the convenience store.

When the kids in my neighborhood wanted a candy bar or a fudgecicle, we had to make a really tough decision: did we really want it bad enough to walk a mile for it? Often we didn't, and stayed home and sulked instead. Looking back, we must have been a sorry, surly bunch.

Mrs. Lopez finally came to our rescue. She lived at the end of the block, several doors down from me, and had three small boys. An overly-protective mom, she hated it when her two older boys asked for permission to walk to a store so far away. At the same time, since the youngest of her sons was still only a few months old, it was difficult for her to just drop what she was doing and take them herself. Thus, the concept of the "Lopez Family Store" was born.

I first learned of the store from the oldest of the Lopez brothers, Robert. He interrupted a game of street football one night to say that his mom was going to open up a candy store in his house, and that the next day we should bring over all of our change.

Of course, nobody believed him. Whoever heard of anyone opening up a store in their house, for crying out loud?

But it was true. Within a few days, every kid in the neighborhood had visited the Lopez residence at least a couple of times. By the end of her first week in business, Mrs. Lopez had successfully emptied the contents of every piggy bank within half a mile.

The den in the Lopez home had been converted into sort of a one-room general store. Mrs. Lopez had found a source for wholesale quantities of our favorite candy bars, from butterfingers to zero bars, and had them neatly laid out on long shelves her husband had made for her. The candy bars were a nickel cheaper than at the "Stop 'n' Go," and didn't require a long walk. We were in kid heaven.

Each time we left her house, we were given the same warning. "Remember, don't tell anybody, or we'll have to close down the store." We each swore to ourselves that we'd keep this secret to our last breath.

Boys in general, I think, feel like secret agents when adults ask them to keep a secret. They conjure up visions of cold war spies, secret handshakes and fast cars with machine guns mounted on their hoods.

Of course, we didn't know at the time why we were asked to keep the store a secret. We didn't know who the "bad guys" were, or why they would make our neighbor shut down her operation. It didn't really matter. We just wanted to continue to use the store, and if keeping a big secret would enable us to do that, we'd play along.

We'd talk at school about the "you know what," and "guess what you-know-who has now?" Of course, before each comment we'd look up and down the halls a couple of times, as though a commie spy was lurking behind the radiator just waiting to learn our secrets. Then we'd reduce our voices to whispers as we'd indulge such sensitive state secrets as the fact that Mrs. Lopez now stocked Hershey bars.

Very quickly, of course, the word got out around the neighborhood, and many of the mothers on our street asked her to stock such things as milk, bread and eggs. It wasn't unusual at all to see some of the neighborhood men shuffling over to the Lopez house early on a Saturday morning, sometimes in bath robes and slippers, and returning home a few minutes later with a quart of milk or package of bacon tucked under one arm.

Eventually, the Lopez family started parking their car in the driveway and expanded their operation into the garage. Instantly, they were able to double their inventory. They were obviously turning a tidy profit.

After a few weeks went by, the store was no longer a secret at all. Back then San Antonio had a neighborhood policing program. Police officers were assigned to particular neighborhoods, and were encouraged to interact with the residents. For that reason, we'd frequently have uniformed members of the San Antonio Police Department park their squad cars at the end of our street and volunteer to be the quarterbacks for our street football games.

It must have been an odd sight for the uninitiated to see these policemen run into Mrs. Lopez' house, buy a soda and an ice cream bar, then climb back into their cars to resume their patrols.

When I moved out of the neighborhood a year later, the little market was still going strong.

Not long ago I drove down Bane Street. I half-expected to see one stream of kids going into the Lopez house, and another stream coming out with candy and other snacks. But I saw neither. Instead, I saw an open garage door and a 1966 Chevy Impala parked where the display shelves once stood. I guess all good things must come to an end sometime...

The Cherry Tree

When I was young and carefree, with much more time on my hands and far fewer concerns, I spent a lot of time doing what my father called "loafing." This was nothing more than floating around the neighborhood, doing nothing in particular, other than enjoying the company of my friends, savoring the wonders of childhood, and generally looking for something to do.

Oh, we generally didn't look that hard. It was just as enjoyable, especially on a nice summer day, to lounge around and talk, as it was to play sports or get into mischief. So I spent a lot of time lying under the small cherry tree in the corner of my back yard. Sometimes my friends would be there, sometimes I'd be alone. But I was never lonesome, sitting there under that tree. Even when there was no one else around, I still had my imagination.

It was in the soft green grass under that tree that I would lie while my daydreams took me around the world in a tricked-out airplane, visiting faraway lands and people who looked and acted nothing like me. I imagined myself on the deck of a three-masted schooner with a pirate's sword in my hand and the Jolly Roger whipping above my head, as I commanded one of my crewmen to walk the plank as punishment for an unknown misdeed.

When the Star Trek series first hit the airways, it was a bust with our parents, but all the kids in the neighborhood loved the show. Under my cherry tree, I was on board the bridge of the starship Enterprise, Captain Kirk's right-hand man, and the one who managed to save the day each time a crisis occurred. Of course, it wasn't until much later, when I saw the show's reruns on a color television, that I realized how truly spectacular the bridge really was.

When my friends were with me under that tree, we talked for hours about Captain Kirk and our other heroes: Mickey Mantle, Don Drysdale, the Mercury astronauts. We'd argue endlessly about whether Mantle was a better all-around ballplayer than Babe Ruth or Lou Gehrig, and what a shame it was that these legends of different generations never had a chance to play one another.

When we weren't talking baseball, we'd watch tiny ants scurrying about, going about the business of gathering food and maintaining their homes. We'd chew on blades of grass, and marvel about how different grasses had sometimes strikingly different tastes. And we'd watch the clouds roll by and daydream about being in outer space, or soaring overhead in a rocket.

We talked a lot about girls, and what a pain in the neck they were. As we grew older, we changed so slowly that we didn't even realize it was happening. One day we woke up and realized that we no longer despised girls, and that they were sometimes fun to be around. Looking back, that's when life really started getting complicated.

There were absolutely no subjects which were off limits. We would talk about old Mrs. Greer, and wonder how horrible her life must have been to turn her into the hideous witch she was. We'd talk about the rumors that ghosts and vampires frequented her house in the late hours when the moon was full. We'd speculate about the number of bodies of dead boys she had buried beneath her rickety old clapboard shack. Each time a casual acquaintance would move from the neighborhood without notice, we'd assume his bones were rotting under Mrs. Greer's floorboards.

I remember one afternoon arguing about George Washington, and whether or not the tale of his chopping down his own cherry tree was fact or fiction. We were pretty much split on whether the story was true, but we did agree on one thing. If it was true, George Washington was a sap. None of us would ever have confessed to cutting down a tree without permission. We realized, of course, that telling a lie was wrong, but it was certainly in order if it kept us from getting our hides tanned.

When the cherries were ripe, and even when they weren't, we'd pluck them off the tree by the handful, eat them, and spit the pits at each other. The cherries on this particular tree were a bit on the sour side, but we didn't mind. We were all from poor families, and these cherries might be the only fresh fruit we'd eat for several days, so we relished every bit.

One year the branches of the tree were covered with tiny worms, and Dennis tore open a cherry with his fingers to discover worms inside the tiny fruit. We picked a couple more and opened them as well, and sure enough, they were similarly infested.

For the next several weeks, Mark had all the cherries he could eat. When he picked a handful and offered us some, we'd pass, saying we had a stomach ache, or had eaten enough earlier, or just weren't in the mood for cherries. Poor Mark never did catch on. Looking back, it occurs to me that adolescent boys can be most cruel to their closest friends. But it was all in the name of good clean fun.

Some years later, when I was in high school, my father cut down that cherry tree. I recently went back to that old house, which is vacant now, and I stood on the very spot where that cherry tree stood so many years ago. I noticed that the ants were still there, busy as ever, completely unaware of my presence. I plucked a blade of grass from the ground where the tree once stood, and found myself wondering why chewing on grass was so appealing to young boys. Perhaps my tastes had grown more sophisticated over the years. Maybe I just lacked the spirit of the young, and that's what made the grass taste so sweet so many years ago. All I knew was, on this particular day and time, the grass was nothing worth bragging about.

The clouds were still there, of course, rolling by above me as I lay in the long grass that has overtaken this particular corner of the yard. The clouds had a calming affect, just as they did when I was ten, and it made me remember how watching these wisps of vapor high in the sky used to make me forget all my troubles. Had I stayed there long enough, I'm sure they'd have done the same thing for me on that particular day.

I've decided that we need to spend more time loafing. Especially the kids of this new millennium, who are so inundated with mp3 players, video games, and high tech computers that they no longer experience the simple pleasures of just being a kid outdoors. We need to put aside their electronic toys occasionally and shove them outside to do what countless generations have done for centuries: get to know and love Mother Nature and her earth. And cherry trees.

The Eye in the Drain

When I was a youngster, I just knew that my house was haunted. And in addition to the usual ghosts and witches, there were monsters lurking about. Every time I turned a corner, or opened a door, I caught the quick glimpse of a shadow, or heard the soft rustle of something scurrying out of sight. What scared me the most, though, and invariably sent an icy shiver up my spine, was the hideous sea monster that lived beneath my bathtub.

My twin sister Debbie and I were playing cards a few years ago when talk turned toward the old house on 32nd Street where we grew up. We were explaining to our young nephew that when we were his age we lived in a house that had no shower, just an old bathtub. And since our family was poor, we didn't have the luxury of having a nightly bath in this tub. The old joke about getting a bath every Saturday night, "whether we needed it or not," really applied to us. We lived it.

When I asked Debbie if she remembered the eyeball in the drain, she looked at me like I was crazy. Then she laughed. She thought I was kidding.

"You don't remember the eye?" I asked in bewilderment. I was looking for some support, a verification that I hadn't imagined the whole thing, a reassurance that I hadn't spent my entire childhood terrified of a monster that didn't really exist.

She looked at me blankly, not knowing whether I was pulling her leg. So I had to explain how I used to peer down the drain of the bathtub while the water drained out. And sometimes, if the angle was right as I gazed through the water and into the drain beneath it, I could see an eyeball peering back up at me from inside the drain. Honest.

As long as the drain was plugged, I had a good time in the tub. I had a toy boat which kept me entertained for hours. In my mind, it was a World War II battleship that belonged to the German navy. I was an American submarine commander, unseen just below the surface of the Atlantic, stalking my prey above me. I would very quietly shadow the ship until the time was just right, then clobber it with imaginary torpedoes. Ka-Blam! I was a sure-shot, scoring direct hits amidships every time. That toy boat was sunk a thousand times in my imaginary ocean.

We had no Mr. Bubble at my house. It was too expensive. From time to time, though, I used dishwashing liquid if it was available, and laundry powder if it wasn't. I preferred the Ivory liquid, because it didn't leave a greasy film on my body the way Tide did.

I always had a blast in the plugged tub, until someone started beating on the door of the bathroom. Since this was the only bathroom in our small house, my pesky sisters had no qualms in pounding on the door in a futile attempt to get me to hurry up. To this day, I'm convinced that they did it out of spite, and not because they actually needed to use the bathroom. But I have to admit I did the same thing to them occasionally.

Sometimes my sisters left me alone, and I was able to soak in the tub until my hands and feet looked like prunes, and turned a snowy white. That's when I knew it was time to get out.

I always dreaded pulling the plug, for I knew it was only a matter of time before that old sea monster decided to pop out of the drain and make a meal of me. I would pull out the plug with some apprehension, then sit at the back of the tub, German battleship in hand, ready to use it as a weapon should the need arise. And more often than not, as the water drained, my curiosity would get the best of me. I'd lean over and peer into the drain to see if the monster was still there. He invariably was. But he always disappeared as soon as the water was finished draining.

When I got a little older, in an effort to convince myself that there really were no monsters which lived under bathtubs, I tried to find a rational explanation for this particular phenomenon. I finally determined that the eyeball was an illusion, which occurred when the swirling water at the mouth of the drain formed a little whirlpool, and either reflected the vision of my own eyeball back at me, or refracted the light from the bare bulb over the tub to create the illusion of an eye.

I should say that in the years since I grew up I tried to duplicate this phenomenon on a couple of occasions, with no success. It may be that the conditions weren't just right, or because the drain was a different size, or because modern drains are covered with stainless steel traps. Or, it might just be that there really was an old sea monster that lived under my bathtub so many years ago...

That's the theory I'm going with. It's better than thinking I might be crazy.

Best Car I Ever Owned

I asked several of my friends the other day which, of all the cars they've owned in their lifetime, brought them the greatest number of pleasant memories. Almost all of them said it was the first car they ever owned, and many of them were so fond of their first cars that they wanted to tell me about them.

I certainly understand how they feel. No matter what it looks like, how old it is, or how well it runs, a boy's first car holds a special place in his heart for a lifetime.

Mine was a Ford, a 1963 Galaxy 500. It was beige in color and wasn't much to look at, but the body was in pretty good shape and it ran like a dream. Although it wasn't one of the "cool" cars that the rich kids drove to Lubbock High School every day, it suited me just fine. It cost $325, which my father loaned me in exchange for a promise that I would do yard work and other chores around the house until I had paid off the debt.

The car was spotless. Never mind that most of the time you couldn't see the floor in my bedroom, and that I wasn't exactly known for my cleanliness. My car was an exception. Not a weekend went by that it didn't get washed. Even in the winter, I pulled into a local car wash every week or so to keep it sparkling.

My friends used to joke that I bought Turtle Wax by the case. To be sure, I tended to use a lot of it. But I liked the way the car gleamed when the sunlight hit it, and it was well worth the hours I spent buffing and polishing.

For a high school senior on a limited budget, there's nothing more frustrating than a car that breaks down. Luckily, my old Ford was born in an era when "backyard mechanics" did most of their own work. I knew how to do most of the repairs, short of an overhaul, and the 1963 Galaxy 500 was splendidly easy to work on.

These days I wouldn't even dream of working on my own car. Even if I could find the broken part under the tangle of hoses and unnecessary accessories under the modern hood, I wouldn't have the proper tools to get it off, or the computer equipment needed to perform diagnostics on it. In my first car, the engine compartment was uncluttered and simple, only containing the minimum number of parts needed to get me where I wanted to go.

I recall fondly the time when my ignition system was going bad and I didn't have the money to buy replacement parts. I learned then that it was possible to start my car with a screwdriver by reaching under the hood and causing an electrical arc across the solenoid.

I also learned that when the temperature is twenty degrees outside, and your windshield is covered with a thick layer of ice, you shouldn't pour hot water on the ice to melt it away. I actually did that once. In my feeble teenage mind, it seemed perfectly logical. The windshield immediately shattered, making me feel like a moron, and leaving me with a dilemma: how to pay $60 for a replacement windshield when I'm only bringing home about $30 a week. Thanks, Dad, for coming to my rescue.

A bigger problem was explaining my stupidity to my family and friends, and I solved that by doing what any other boy would do in the same situation. I lied. I told them that my heater hose broke and sprayed hot water from under the hood onto the windshield. To my amazement, they bought it.

It was while I was in school that Texas stopped issuing new license plates every year. Under their new system, each year when it was time to renew your registration, you paid the fee and the state sent you a little sticker to place on the corner of your license plate. At the time, I thought it was insanity not to issue new plates every year, but since every state in the union now uses the sticker method, or something similar to it, I guess Texas was just ahead of its time.

Anyway, in 1977 I didn't have a lot of money to spend (some things never change), so when I discovered that my registration had expired, I panicked. I decided that since I didn't have the money to renew it, and I couldn't stop driving my pride and joy, that I would put my high school art lessons to a practical use. I would make my own sticker. I cut out a small piece of red construction paper, painted a "77" on it with white model paint, and a few other squiggly lines that from a distance (I thought) made it look like a real registration sticker. A bit of rubber cement, and it looked good enough to pass until I could afford to get a real sticker.

I didn't expect to get stopped for speeding a few days later.

I was pulled over by a motorcycle cop on 19th Street, in front of Texas Tech University. He walked up to my window, told me I was going ten miles over the limit, and asked to see my driver's license. Then he went to the back of my car to check my license plate.

I thought my goose was cooked when the policeman walked back to my window. I was wondering now many years I'd be spending in jail. But he didn't say a word about my artwork. Instead, he asked where my eyeglasses were.

"Huh?" I asked. He explained. "Your license says you have to wear corrective lenses. Do you wear contact lenses?"

There was no end to my stupidity. "Uh, yes," I lied. "I am wearing contact lenses."

He leaned over to look into my eyes as I fidgeted nervously in my seat. After what seemed like an eternity, he said, "Well, okay. I'm going to let you off with a warning for speeding..."

All right! I'm sure I breathed a very loud sigh of relief, thinking I had outsmarted the cop and gotten away with everything. It was at that very moment I looked in my rearview mirror and saw another cop walking up behind the car.

"Whatcha got there, Bob, some kinda comedian or something?"

I sank into the seat in a deep state of despair as the newcomer took the first cop back for a closer inspection of my license plate. Then they returned, handed me my little red sticker, and told me to pull my car into an adjacent parking lot and park it.

There must have been a rule in the Lubbock Police Department that prevented their officers from displaying a sense of humor in the 1970s.

They did give me a ride home. It was the least they could do for the $105 in fines I had to pay...

Doc McKenzie

I miss the whole concept of a family doctor. In these days of assembly-line medicine and HMOs, what too many families have instead is a medical factory, where they take their sick children and place them on a conveyor belt to be seen by the next available physician. Or physician's assistant. Or nurse practitioner. Thank you very much, pay at the door, don't call me in the morning.

A couple of things about this bother me. First of all, when you walk into one of these places, you don't know whether you're going to be seen by Marcus Welby, M.D., or a pimple-faced kid fresh out of medical school who calls you "sir" because you look like his grandfather.

The other thing that bothers me about this new style of medicine is the lack of a bond between doctor and patient. Hand in hand with this missing bond is a lack of trust. When families had physicians of their own, they grew to trust them and rely on them to keep the family healthy. They were comfortable with the physician. The physician called them by their first name, and knew their dog's name, and knew not only their medical history, but their family history as well. We as a society lost something when family doctors started getting replaced by managed care.

A generation ago, the family doctor was also a close family friend. In the smaller towns across the country, these physicians delivered not only most of the children in town, but many of their parents as well. They knew which of their patients were predisposed to certain diseases, because they treated their parents for those diseases.

Perhaps more important, they knew their patients well enough to recognize them on the street, call out their names, and wave to them. They sat next to their patients at church, and knew their hopes and dreams as well as their bad eating habits.

Old Doc McKenzie worked out of an old house on 34th Street, just west of Avenue Q, in my hometown of Lubbock.

The house was tall and haughty, a proud Victorian built in the late 1800s with money from the cattle industry that helped the town develop. But its glory days were long gone by the first time I entered the house for the first time. To a young kid like me, its history meant nothing. I just found it a little bit intimidating.

Inside the house's front room sat the receptionist, who did the preliminary interview and screening. I can't remember her name, but I can picture her face as though she were sitting next to me today: a bit plain, yet pretty, with the brightly colored eye shadow common with twenty-something girls in the sixties, friendly, caring, concerned. She always promised the kids a sucker on the way out, provided she got a good report from the doctor that they'd behaved themselves. She always made good on the promise, no matter how much the kid pitched a fit about being there.

Doc McKenzie was a stately gentleman, tall, with a full head of gray hair. He had a distinguished look about him, and if he weren't so well known in the community might have been mistaken for a politician or a judge. Many of his patients were students at nearby Texas Tech College (that was before it became a "university"). They went to him because he was reliable, knew what he was doing, and was reasonably priced. I suppose that's why my family went to him as well.

I liked Doc McKenzie because he didn't treat me like a kid. That is to say, he didn't talk down to me like I was an idiot. None of this "...and how are you doing in school, little boy?" stuff. He talked to me like he talked to my father. That had a way of making me feel grown up and somehow important.

Conversely, there were certain things I didn't like about going to see Doc McKenzie.

Aside from the house itself, which I just knew had to be haunted, and which creaked and groaned as you walked its interior, was the fact that old Doc was always pointing out to my father that my immunizations were out of date. I suppose I should be grateful to him for ensuring that I never got polio or the measles, but it's hard for me to forgive him for the pain his shots caused me. I, like every other kid I ever knew, hated shots with a passion. I'd rather fall off my bike at full speed, skin up both elbows and both knees, and crack my skull on the pavement, than get a shot.

Well, maybe not, but I did hate to get shots. It wasn't until years later, when I was in the military, I learned that the trick to getting a shot is to watch the needle go in. Turns out it's the not the shot itself that hurts, it's the not-knowing of when it's coming. I learned many years later that if you watch the whole process, it doesn't hurt at all, or at least very little.

I often went to Doc McKenzie's when my brother Randy or one of my sisters was being treated. I usually hung out in the parking lot or snuck next door to the Enco station to get a nickel's worth of peanuts from their vending machine. There were frequently other siblings there as well, and we'd play hide and seek or marbles, or gaze at the upstairs windows of the old house and try to catch the ghosts behind the sheer curtains peering back down at us.

I thought the family doctor had gone the way of the horse and buggy, but a friend told me not long ago that there are still a few practicing in some of the small towns across America. I envy their patients, and their ability to develop a long-term relationship with their family doctors. I hope they survive the move to push managed health care onto every American. Unfortunately for me, old Doc McKenzie now lives only in my memory...

Game? What Game?

I learned during my sophomore year in high school that there are a hundred things you can do underneath the bleachers during a high school basketball game, and few have anything to do with the game itself.

My friends and I used to sneak beneath the bleachers shortly before the game started, when the fans were milling about, making their way to and from the restrooms and the refreshment stand, or looking around for acquaintances.

The bleachers themselves were the folding variety, which laid flat against the walls of the gymnasium when not in use. Shortly before the game, the maintenance crew would pull them out to within five feet of the court line, where they would accommodate several hundred spectators on each side of the gym. The south bleachers belonged to the students and fans of my alma mater, Lubbock High School, while the north bleachers hosted the fans of whatever school we were playing that night.

The underside of the bleachers, because of the way they were constructed, was a maze of heavy steel support beams and guy wires. It was just dark enough for a small group of teenage boys to hide relatively easily.

Oh, it wasn't without its hazards, and we all bore the occasional bruises and scrapes as proof. But an occasional contusion was well worth the fun we had.

Beneath and to the front of each seat was a plank of wood which ran from the bottom of the seat to within six inches of the step below it. From underneath the bleachers, we saw mostly ankles and shoes through these six inch windows to the world. But we also saw just enough of the game to know what was going on.

Our antics differed according to which set of bleachers we were under. On our own side of the gym, we spent a lot of time listening, trying to recognize voices, with the intent of victimizing certain people. A lot of people knew we were down there, but most kept it to themselves because they knew most of our shenanigans were done in good humor. Of course, catching someone totally off guard was always a special treat.

The snack bar in those days sold fountain drinks in paper cups. A large number of the fans placed their cups at their feet when they weren't actually drinking, so that on those rare occasions when our team did something great, and they stood to their feet, they wouldn't spill their drinks.

Problem was, when that cup was next to their feet, it was temporarily out of their line of sight. We found that by poking a hole in the cup an inch above the fluid line with a six penny nail, we'd create a trap for our unwitting victim. The cup would not leak while sitting on the step, but as soon as the fan picked it up and leaned it toward himself, he'd get a chest full of his favorite soft drink.

We pulled this stunt at least five times on James Sloan. He never did catch on. He'd just rant and rave about the stupid snack bar, and how they never had decent cups. It never dawned on him that the cup didn't leak ten minutes before, when the fluid level was above the mysterious hole. Perhaps this was the reason James skipped rocket science as a career, and chose to drive a beer truck instead.

Of course, there were other equally juvenile pranks we also pulled, like gently tucking lit cigarettes into fans' socks, and placing thumbtacks in various seats before the game began, and tying shoelaces together. We sometimes tied the shoes of different people together. Once, over the course of half an hour, Mark succeeded in loosely tying the laces of six people together, so that when they got up to leave, they discovered they formed a human chain, bound at the ankles.

Carlton had some deer scent he used to get from his dad's hunting cabinet. It consisted mainly of urine from an adult doe, and was used by hunters to spread around the forest to attract bucks. Why the males would be attracted was beyond us, because this was the most god-awful stuff any of us had ever smelled. We poured it liberally over the shoes of visiting fans when we were under their bleachers. We waited until the game was almost over, though, so we wouldn't have to smell it any longer than we had to in our confined space.

We once had a referee call two technical fouls on a visiting team, because we kept blowing a whistle from underneath the team's bleachers. The referees said it was interfering with the game, and warned the visiting team's coach repeatedly to tell his fans to knock it off. The poor coach would dutifully look into the stands in an effort to quiet the offender, but because of the gymnasium's tendency to echo, no one knew exactly where the whistle was coming from. Except us, of course. We only stopped when the referee threatened to call the game.

Mark had a Daisy bb pistol that was too underpowered to use for bird hunting. We considered it useless until he brought it to a game one night. These days, sneaking a bb gun onto a school campus would be grounds for expulsion, but those were much simpler (and safer) times. He used the gun to shoot the helium balloons that a visiting team's cheerleaders were passing out to the crowd. When he shot their head cheerleader in the ass, however, we decided he was walking onto thin ice and we talked him into putting the gun away. We told him if he ever brought it again, we were going to hold him down, take off his pants, and throw them into the crowd. He didn't bring it again. As for the cheerleader, boy, was she mad.

We once managed to get under the bleachers at Monterey High School, on the other side of the city. They were our arch rivals, and we took particular delight in sneaking in a large catfish wrapped in plastic wrap and hidden in the sleeve of Mark's jacket. Of course, the fish stayed behind when we left that evening, and I understand it took the janitorial staff several days to find the source of our aromatic gift.

Today, when I attend a high school basketball game, I make a point to check my seat before I sit down, and my shoelaces when I get up to leave. After all, I know that some things never change, and that a new generation of teenage boys may well have discovered how much fun it can be to pay for a basketball game but not watch it.

The Quarry

In south San Antonio, not far from the house where I lived when I was young, lies an old quarry in the middle of 600 acres of Texas scrub brush. Surrounded on three sides by housing developments, this plot of undeveloped land is protected more or less by three sad strands of rusted barbed wire and sporadic signs warning trespassers to keep out.

Most trespassers heed the warnings and stay away. After all, there doesn't seem to be much within this piece of land to draw anyone in for a closer inspection. But my friends Glen and Tommy and I, some forty-odd years ago, got bored one afternoon and decided to climb over the fence. That's how I know about the old quarry.

This was one of the few times when Glen and Tommy and I weren't looking to get into mischief. We'd had our fair share of trouble that summer, which included breaking old lady Morales' dining room window with an errant baseball a few days before on Abacus Street. Back then, we tended to avoid having to accept responsibility for such incidents whenever we could. When the ball shattered the window, we took off so fast that Glen left behind his brand new baseball glove.

We laid low and avoided Abacus Street for several days. This meant we had to take the scenic route when we went to Robert's house, but we didn't mind. We knew that if we walked past Mrs. Morales' house she'd come out and yell at us about being irresponsible and demand money that we didn't have. So, we resigned ourselves to going out of our way until she forgot our faces and the trouble blew over.

Problem was, this also meant we couldn't visit any of our other friends who also lived on Abacus Street. When Robert went on summer vacation with his folks, there were just the three of us. And one day we got very bored. So we climbed over the fence and went exploring.

We really didn't expect to find anything beyond the barbed wire. We merely wanted to check out the area, and maybe run across some skunks or armadillos, or find a scorpion's nest so we could catch some to terrify our sisters with. Since that's the best we expected to find, we were pleasantly surprised to stumble across a fairly good-sized pond.

This pond sat in the middle of a clearing about twice its two-acre size, and completely surrounded by thick mesquite trees. From fifty yards away, it was completely hidden behind this thick blanket of thorny underbrush. What a perfect place to play hooky.

We walked around the water line, trying to determine whether there were fish in the pond. We found a couple of mud-caked old floats and a tangled length of fishing line that told us someone else had been there quite some time before us, and that they'd had the same question.

We walked on, another hundred yards through the brush, and came to a second barbed wire fence. The first one hadn't stopped us, so there was no reason for this one to either. Over we went, curious now why the seemingly unnecessary second fence was there, and what it was protecting.

Another fifty yards, and we came to a place where the brush was exceedingly thick. We had to fight our way through it, but we had gone so far by that time that we were determined to see if there was anything on the other side of it.

Tommy clawed his way through a large shrub, and upon bursting through the other side, almost fell head first into a deep pit. Needless to say, this got our immediate attention.

We stood at the rim of this massive hole in the ground, looking down at the rainwater that had collected at the bottom. The water was an emerald green, and would have been worth exploring further had it not been so inaccessible.

We walked around the pit and pressed farther into the brush, and finally came to a huge clearing. From this point we discovered the massive quarry, and through a boy's eyes it was a magical sight to see. From the amount of dust that covered all the equipment, it was apparent to us that the quarry was seldom worked. That knowledge emboldened us, and gave us the courage to wander freely around the site.

Since the ground was relatively soft, we guessed that the area was mined for its gravel or sand. Still, when Tommy mentioned that he thought it was a gold mine, our rationality went out the window as we searched the ground for sparkling gold nuggets. Then we gave up and decided that whatever these massive earth-moving vehicles moved, it was of no value to us.

The site itself was, though. We climbed aboard the various pieces of equipment and pretended to operate them. If the keys had been in the ignitions, we wouldn't have pretended.

We climbed up a conveyor system which stretched over the largest of the pits, and dared Tommy to jump into the water forty feet below us. Tommy wasn't the brightest guy in the world, and ordinarily might have taken our dare. Luckily, he chose not to on that particular day. We later found out that the water below was only three feet deep. Had he jumped that day, it probably would have been the last thing he'd ever do.

After a couple of hours, we grew tired of the quarry and headed back. But we visited the area again and again that summer and the next. The equipment seldom moved between our visits, and we were always able to waste away an afternoon at the site. We also visited the pond several times to fish. We never caught anything, but it didn't matter. Just being there was easily the biggest part of the adventure.

I've wondered many times over the years if that quarry is still in operation. If you drive down Zaragoza Road in San Antonio today, the nondescript entrance to this place leaves no clues to recent vehicle traffic. In fact, it isn't even marked. Perhaps it's been abandoned, and has turned into a permanent hideaway for the boys in my old neighborhood.

Maybe they'll have better luck with the fish.

Definitely an Acquired Taste

Virtually all kids run with their mouths open. Logic would dictate that they'd keep their mouths clamped tightly shut when running, to keep out pesky flying critters and other unpleasant surprises. But, as I've said many times before, kids are neither logical, nor practitioners of common sense. Hence, they run with their mouths open. Watch them. You'll see.

I suppose they do this because it's easier to inhale large quantities of air for their lungs. Or maybe they just enjoy feeling that satisfying little "crunch" whenever they bite down on an occasional mosquito or gnat that has had the misfortune of flying between their molars.

I used to have a friend named Wesley who actually bragged about eating bugs. But that's a story for another time.

Anyway, to get to the point: for whatever reason, kids run with their mouths open. This can sometimes lead to problems, especially when the running activity is combined with other factors, like nighttime and poor lighting. And cow manure.

Times have changed, and fertilizer technology has advanced a lot since the early 1960s. These days, you can get scientifically engineered, synthetic fertilizer, rich and with just the right minerals and chemicals to turn your lawn a dark rich green overnight. Back then, though, the best way to turn your lawn green was to cover it with a thin layer of something else dark and rich: processed cow manure.

Cow manure today is generally sold in fifty pound bags. That was also an option when I was five. But it was much cheaper by the ton, and my father was always one to take advantage of a bargain whenever he could.

That's how it came to pass that in the spring of 1964, when I was five years old, there happened to be a very large mound of cow manure occupying the middle of our front lawn.

Dad's plan was simple. He'd have the dump truck drop the load in the front yard, and he'd use a wheelbarrow to tote the fertilizer into the back yard, where he'd use it to cover the grass. Then he'd do the same in the front yard, until he ended up with a very small pile. He'd then take a rake and spread out the last of it, to fertilize the spot where the pile laid. A great plan.

The porch light on our front porch burned out about that same time. Since the nearest streetlight was at the corner of the block, that plunged our front yard into almost total darkness on a moonless night.

A five-year old boy, when he's playing G.I. Joe with his friends, running through neighborhood yards in the dark, yelling "bang bang, you're dead," sometimes forgets things. Like the location of a pile of fertilizer.

As I mentioned before, young boys tend to run with their mouths open.

I distinctly remember hitting the fertilizer pile at full speed, and falling face-first into the middle of it. I also recall getting a good-sized mouthful of the stuff, and spending a couple of minutes trying to get rid of it. First by gagging, then by spitting. Many, many times.

I learned several lessons about eating cow manure that night, and all these lessons are still with me today. First of all, one taste is enough. It's not something I want to try again in this lifetime, or the next.

Second, it's a taste that's very hard to get rid of. Even after brushing my teeth and rinsing my mouth out numerous times, I remember tasting it for days afterward.

Last, but not least, when you munch a mouthful of manure, your friends will tease you unmercifully for a long, long time. I never told anyone in my family about "the manure incident." I didn't want to be the butt of their jokes for months or years to come. Although my little brother Randy would become a constant companion in later years, on this particular night he was safely in the house, still too young to be playing outside after dark.

Oddly enough, the memory of my falling into the manure pile isn't an unpleasant one. It is one of my earliest childhood memories, and what I remember most is the joy of running through the darkness, the cool wind blowing on my face, and playing happily with my friends. Those pleasant memories far outweigh the unpleasantness of the event with which I wound up that particular evening.

By the way, I don't use manure to turn the grass green. This is partly because I prefer to buy my fertilizer by the bag instead of the ton. Also, because the scent of cow manure sends a cold shiver up my spine and contorts my face into that of a man who's just bit into something terribly bitter. And it's also because I don't want my grandchildren to learn what cow manure tastes like.

Mrs. Greer

Every street has one: a wrinkled old prune who spends his or her life eavesdropping on others, whose window curtains flutter almost constantly throughout the day, as people come and go, unaware that they're being watched. Back when I was a kid, the term "busybody" was commonly used to describe such people, who were almost invariably old women.

No, I'm not sexist. I'm just stating a fact. In my neighborhood, they really were almost always women. On the rare occasions when a man had the same annoying habits, he had his own name: a "grouchy old man."

On my street, my family and I were unfortunate enough to know this woman all too well, for she was the lady who lived next door to us. Mrs. Greer said perhaps half a dozen words to me during the ten years or so I knew her.

She had a gaze that she directed at me, and all the other children in the neighborhood, that made it perfectly clear that she hated all children, had nothing to say, and didn't want us to waste her time. So we generally didn't. There were many kids on our street who swore that Mrs. Greer was a witch.

Dennis Bryant, who lived on the other side of me and was one of my best friends in the early 1960s, used to swear that she made his skin crawl every time she peeked out at us through her white lace curtains. We all knew very well that we were under constant surveillance by this woman. One day Dennis and I were playing catch in my front yard, when he missed a ball and it rolled down Mrs. Greer's driveway between my house and hers.

While I waited, Dennis walked up the driveway as Mrs. Greer watched from her perch in the front window. As soon as Dennis walked out of her view, she got up, walked through her house to a side window, and followed his movements from a new vantage point. Then, once he had the ball and returned to the front yard, she likewise returned to her original position in her front window. It was an eerie feeling, knowing that we were almost constantly watched any time we were outdoors.

My mother used to say that Mrs. Greer was just a lonely old woman who had nothing better to do than sit in her window and watch the world pass her by. Mom also said that Mrs. Greer's children were grown, and had given her no grandchildren to spend time with her, and that she just watched the neighborhood children because she longed for youngsters of her own. We didn't buy it for a minute.

Perhaps it was because boys will always prefer a gruesome, if less plausible, explanation for any situation. Or maybe it was because Mrs. Greer rebuffed all the neighbors' efforts to be hospitable, even refusing to answer the door when someone's mom went calling with a fresh baked pie or cookies. Whatever the reason, we preferred to believe that Mrs. Greer was a hideous old monster who was unsociable to everyone, and who hated kids in particular.

Mrs. Greer's hostility was adopted by her cats, who were the only living things we ever saw her show affection to. We would occasionally walk into my back yard to see her sitting on her back porch, in a broad galvanized steel lawn chair the color of under ripe olives with snow white handles. She'd sometimes be holding and petting one or both of her cats, who as far as we knew had no names. As soon as she noticed us, she would grab her cats and scurry back into the black dungeon that was her home, a self-imposed prisoner retreating into the dark recesses of a self-made hell.

The larger of the cats, an unkempt tabby, would spend time on top of the four-foot picket fence that separated my yard from its owner's. It would pace back and forth, scowling at us as we played our little boy games. Any attempt to get friendly with this feline would immediately raise his suspicions, and he would stop in his tracks and try to beat us back with a decidedly wicked look. I once took a dare and tried to get close enough to pet him. I almost made it before he arched his back, hissed an angry warning to me, and took off in the opposite direction.

The smaller of the cats, a scrawny calico, sometimes climbed to the top of my garage. I spent a lot of time there in my youth, contemplating life and watching the clouds roll by from a position mostly covered by the branches of an old elm tree. This cat, although a bit more bold, was no more friendly, and similarly resisted all efforts to show affection to him, and more than once scratched the heck out my arms and hands.

The last time I saw Mrs. Greer was when her daughter and son in law put her into the back seat of their car one day and drove her off to an old folks' home. Ronnie's father told him that she had gotten too old and senile to live by herself. In our view she should have been taken away years before.

Once she was gone, her cats began wandering the neighborhood for occasional meals, and spent much of their time digging through garbage cans in the alley behind our house. Perhaps they, left to fend for themselves in a miserable world that neither wanted them nor was willing to care for them, weren't too different from Mrs. Greer herself.

Lubbockisms

I was born and raised in west Texas. I used to think that this part of our great country was unique for its idiosyncratic habits, which I had seen in no other place on the planet. But eventually I learned that every locale has its own such habits. They seem perfectly normal to the locals, but absolutely weird to outsiders.

There are literally hundreds of examples. Go to Phoenix and complain about the 112 degree temperature, and you'll likely hear the comment "yes, but it's a dry heat."

Oh. That makes me feel cooler already. Thanks a lot.

People in the south suck on crayfish, which aren't really fish at all, and which are called "crawdads" by the locals. New Yorkers, in the south on vacation, run from these little lobster-like creatures.

Many Michiganders swim in icy river water in the winter, calling it "refreshing." I call it "pneumonia waiting to happen."

Hawaiians have a hand sign that they flash to one another on the street. With their pinky and thumb extended, and their other fingers tucked in, they wave their hand from side to side as a greeting. It means "hang loose." I lived in Honolulu for three years when I was younger, and never saw anyone hanging, loosely or otherwise.

I suppose it's not surprising, then, that my hometown of Lubbock, Texas has its own share of idiosyncrasies. Some of them are shared with other parts of the country. For example, lunch is called "dinner," while the evening meal is called "supper." This is generally true throughout most of the south.

Also in Lubbock, stop signs are merely a suggestion. This tradition was started many years ago by Texas Tech University students, and was gradually picked up by the rest of the citizenry. Today, anyone who has the gall to actually stop at a stop sign is treated to a barrage of unfriendly hand signals and verbiage from the guy in the car behind him. The Lubbock Police Department long ago gave up on trying to cite drivers for this particular type of infraction. They consider anyone who slows down to ten miles an hour at a stop sign an above-average driver.

Another thing Lubbockites do, when they meet a stranger from somewhere else, is mention both Buddy Holly and Mac Davis within the first twenty seconds of the conversation. As in "Oh, you're from Albuquerque? Have you been to the Buddy Holly museum? Go right up University Avenue to Broadway. Mac Davis' father used to run a motel on University. You'll pass it on your way."

I suppose it's only natural that a city would be proud of its most famous former residents, so I can't fault anyone for this habit. These days, though, there seems to be a growing number of visitors who walk away from the conversation wondering "Buddy who?"

Every Lubbockite has used the adage "If you don't like the weather, hang around ten minutes and it'll change," at least once. Invariably, this is followed by uproarious laughter, as the speaker is genuinely impressed with his own wit. You'd think he'd written the words himself. I've heard the same adage in at least ten other states and three other countries.

For some reason, Lubbockites refer to their hometown newspaper, the Lubbock Avalanche-Journal, as the "A-J." I find this peculiar in light of the fact that many newspapers have hyphenated names, but their readers don't generally reduce their paper's name to a set of initials. Honoluluans do not refer to their Star-Bulletin as the "S-B." Residents of Atlanta do not call the office of the Journal-Constitution and say "I want to subscribe to the J-C."

Go to a newsstand in Dallas and try it for yourself. Ask the vendor for a copy of the "M-N." He'll likely tell you he doesn't sell candy. Then he'll offer you a copy of the Morning News.

Probably the most peculiar habit I've seen fellow Lubbockites do is put peanuts in a bottle of coke while they drink it.

By the way, the term "coke" in Lubbock is frequently substituted for the word "soda," and used for any soft drink, regardless of the brand or flavor. It's not unusual to overhear the following conversation: "Go to the store and get me a coke, will ya?" "Sure, what kind?" "A root beer."

Anyway, back to the peanuts. When you pour them into a bottle of soda, they sink to the bottom, give the drink a slightly salty flavor, and provide a snack when the drink is finished.

This particular habit has been around for decades. I saw my father and his brothers drop their peanuts into their cokes a thousand times. I did it for years myself. Many old-timers still do it, and have passed it on to the kids of today. The last time I was in Lubbock I saw a boy of about ten in a 7-Eleven who bought a bag of salted red peanuts and a Dr. Pepper, then poured the peanuts into the bottle. That could have been me forty years ago.

I've decided that these peculiar habits are a good thing. They make each of our hometowns unique, allow us to dredge up old memories and give us a reason to smile and poke fun at ourselves. I will never understand, though, how anybody can intentionally bring themselves to suck on a crawdad.

The Theater

I recently took my granddaughter to one of those shoe box-sized theaters at the local mall... the ones that hold about 20 movie-goers. We were there to see "Twilight."

While waiting for the movie to start, I told her that I was about her age the first time I went to see a movie, and that the theater I went to was big enough to hold all the people in all of the mall's theaters combined.

"All the theaters?" she asked incredulously. The look on her face told me that she wasn't sure if I was telling the truth or pulling her leg.

"Yep," I said. "All the theaters." Her face changed to a look that clearly showed she thought I had lost my mind.

The Village Theater was on 34th Street in Lubbock, exactly halfway between my house and the elementary school. It was a grand theater, with beige velvet-covered walls and bright red carpeting, and a doorman who helped you inside, tore your ticket in half and *sincerely* asked you to enjoy the movie.

At the Village, popcorn tasted like popcorn was supposed to taste. Long before anybody realized that extra butter could kill, they ladled it on by the cup. Salt? Sure! Buckets of it.

A box of candy was 25 cents, and was big enough to share with your friends. It looked nothing like the anorexic boxes of candy theaters sell today at $3.50 apiece.

The first movie I saw at the Village was a full-length Disney cartoon called "The Jungle Book." I don't remember much about the movie today, and I think that's because the theater made a bigger impression on me than the movie did.

I visited that theater many times during my childhood. Many a rainy Saturday, my friends and I would spend all day at the Village, watching the same movie over and over again. The theater management in those days believed that if you were a paying customer, you deserved to be treated like one. Even if you were just a kid. If you wanted to watch the movie a second time, or a third or a fourth time, then you should be able to do so. That kind of customer service doesn't exist in any of the theaters I've been to lately.

It was at the Village that we first saw "The Planet of The Apes." At the time, it was a science-fiction masterpiece, and told a great story without violence, sex, or millions of dollars' worth of special effects. It's still one of my favorite movies.

The theater occasionally ran promotions, which allowed them to give a small toy to kids when they played certain movies. When my friends and I saw "The Blob," we were each given a plastic egg containing a putty-like substance at the ticket window. That was a mistake on the theater's part. By the end of the movie, we'd run out of putty after spending an hour and a half breaking it into small pieces and throwing it across the theater at each other.

Sometimes, the manager would let us run across the street to Griff's Hamburger Stand to get a quick burger, then let us back in to watch the movie a second or third time. Try finding a theater manager anywhere today who will grant this small courtesy.

Two or three times each summer, when we were mowing lawns and alleys for extra pocket money, the theater manager would let us mow the alley behind the Village for free admission. He'd throw in free popcorn and a coke, and sometimes a box of candy. After fighting with a lawnmower in 100-plus degree heat, sitting in the cool theater with an icy drink and a good movie to watch qualified as a young boy's heaven.

Many years ago, the Village Theater was converted to an indoor batting cage business, catering to little league players and softball teams who want to improve their batting averages. Unfortunately, things don't always change for the better. The parking lot next to the theater is now covered with a self-service car wash. Across the street, a fast-food taco joint has replaced Griff's.

Several times I've been tempted to walk into the building, pick up a bat, and take a few swings while looking around to see how the place has changed on the inside. But I think it would break my heart. I think I'm just better off remembering the Village the way it used to be.

How *Not* To Coach Baseball

My little league career lasted only two seasons, before I lost interest and moved on to other pursuits. I was an average player on an average team. When I signed up, I knew that I'd get to wear a sharp uniform, and get to play at the local ball field, in front of a crowd of people who would cheer for me when I made a good play.

I was just naïve enough to forget all the long, monotonous practice sessions, the abusive coaches, and the fans who could be particularly brutal when a young batter got caught watching the third strike sail over the plate.

Don't get me wrong. I thoroughly enjoyed the game. It's just that I wanted every day to be a game day, and I wanted to hit a home run in every game. I thought that practices, where we spent endless hours retrieving shagged balls, were a monumental waste of time.

To make it worse, my coaches had little tolerance for the four or five of us on the team who showed little interest in practice. We were the "slackers" who needed to shape up if we wanted any playing time, they said.

Oh, we worked as hard as anyone else did. We had to, because we had an equal share of balls hit our way that we had to snag and throw back. But because we weren't enthusiastic about doing this inane drill for three straight hours, we were given the "slacker" tag and treated like mutts.

It didn't help that the head coach's son, Johnny, was the biggest slacker of all. And that he had very little natural talent. And that he was our team's starting pitcher. And closer. A couple of others on the team would have liked to have the opportunity to pitch a time or two, but since Johnny had a lock on the pitcher's mound they knew they'd never get a chance.

The other two coaches' sons had similar locks on the first base and shortstop positions. The rest of us were doomed to spend the season rotating in and out of the other positions, the ones no one really wanted.

The fact that Johnny was a slacker frustrated his father tremendously. Johnny complained to us that his dad wanted him to show "leadership," so that the rest of us would follow him blindly through the long practices, obeying commands like sheep because Johnny was setting the example for us.

Johnny had no interest in leadership. He, like us, merely wanted to play the game and have fun. He also confided to us out of earshot of his dad that he wasn't crazy about pitching. He did it because his dad was head coach and told him he had to. He said he'd rather be the catcher, because the catcher's mask was cool and because he wanted to clobber runners sliding into home.

In essence, we all discovered that year that little league baseball wasn't all that different than school. We all had assignments to do and places to fill and instructions to follow. It didn't matter if we agreed with it, or enjoyed it. We did what we were told to do. Fun didn't factor in to the equation.

We, the slackers, were chewed out unmercifully at every practice, punished for our lack of enthusiasm by running endless laps, and tasked at the end of each practice to collect all the bats and balls.

I remember one particularly brutal practice on a particularly hot day, when the coach refused to give the slackers any water after practice because we hadn't "worked hard enough." We'd had just as many balls hit to us as the rest of the team, and had dutifully caught each one and thrown them back. But somehow in his mind we weren't carrying our share of the load. So, our punishment was to stand in the sweltering heat and wither away from dehydration.

Bear in mind, those were the days long before bottled water. The only water available was from the five-gallon thermos the coach brought with him. Denied that, we became parched very quickly.

I distinctly remember how beaten and defeated I felt when I left practice that day. I wanted to quit, but was determined not to let the coach have the satisfaction. Ronnie McCullough and I collapsed onto a stranger's lawn while walking home that day, cupping our hands to gather water from a puddle and sipping it, and letting a water sprinkler soak us, until we'd gathered the energy to get up and stumble the rest of the way home.

During games, we slackers sat on the bench most of the time. Johnny was the exception, of course, and he and the players who'd won the coach's favor took the field. Mind you, most of them were no better than we were. None of them worked any harder than we did, but because they were related to the coaches, or to the coaches' bosses or neighbors, or because they kissed the coaches' butts, they were granted priority when taking the field.

We'd spend most of our time passively watching the game, and waiting for one of the other two or three slackers on the field to drop an easy fly ball, or miss a tag, or swing at a high and outside pitch. Those things would infuriate the coach enough to make him yell at the transgressor, take him out of the game, and replace him with another bench warmer.

As we waited our turn to get into the game, we spent time talking about girls, the meaning of life, and making up very crude jokes about the coach and his mom. It seemed to be our right to do so, and the only chance we had to feel a small degree of vengeance.

As I said, I was an average player on an average team. I distinctly remember the first time I struck out, and the sick feeling I felt in the pit of my stomach. I also remember my first home run, both for the way it made me feel and because it was one of the few times the coach ever said a kind word to me.

Johnny eventually became a pretty good ballplayer, played in high school, and won an athletic scholarship. That was his ticket to a college education he might not have had otherwise. But I always wondered if it was worth all the years of being pushed into doing something he only passively enjoyed.

I learned a valuable lesson that baseball season. I learned that, at least in our league, anyone could be a little league coach. It didn't require a sense of sportsmanship, or fair play, or even a lot of knowledge. All it required was someone who was willing to take charge of 17 boys and spend 20 hours a week with them.

Years later I coached a little league team for one of my sons, and I tried to apply some of the lessons I learned from my own experiences. On my team everyone got a chance to play just as much as my son. All players were of equal importance, and we had no "slackers." The one thing Johnny's dad taught me so many years ago was just as important as knowing how to coach. He taught me how *not* to, and I was able to apply that to my son's team. I suppose it was a valuable lesson in a way. My son's team won the league championship two years in a row.

My experience with Johnny's dad and my other coaches taught me that coaching is about caring and teaching kids, and not yelling at them or abusing them. Wherever my coaches are today, I hope they're watching the games from the bleachers and leaving the coaching to those who are better suited for it.

The Lake

I'd driven by it more than a dozen times. Something seemed vaguely familiar about this small lake on State Highway 380 in Brownfield, Texas, but I just couldn't put my finger on it.

Part of a city park, this lake was surrounded by tall shade trees and overrun with over-friendly ducks and geese, a combination of Canadians and grays, who survived by mooching bread and potato chips from picnickers, school children and passers-by.

When I lived in Alamogordo, New Mexico, just a few years ago, I used this route often. I traveled through Brownfield on my way to and from Post, Texas, where my children lived. Every time I drove through the city of Brownfield, I would gaze upon that lake and wonder why I had the feeling I'd been there before.

I finally realized the significance of this park one summer day when I was taking Chris and Jennifer back to New Mexico with me and they convinced me we should stop to feed the ducks. We first visited a local grocery store, where we got a full-sized loaf of *Rainbo* bread.

When we pulled into the park and drove around the dirt road surrounding the lake, I saw for the first time the earthen levee dividing not one, but two small lakes. Suddenly it hit me like a ton of bricks: this is the lake we visited on our way to El Paso in 1964.

The first family vacation I can ever remember was a long, meandering journey which took us from our home in Lubbock through Brownfield, into the Big Bend area of Texas, then to El Paso, across the border into Juarez, Mexico, and eventually to Carlsbad, New Mexico. One of my vague memories of that trip was a park where we'd stopped to feed the ducks and take photographs. *This* was that park.

The park had remained in my memory for several reasons. The most vivid part of my recollection was always the pleasure of feeding the ducks. Although I've had the opportunity to feed similar birds at many different places in the years since, the 1964 trip was my first experience with this simple pleasure, and it had branded itself permanently in my memory. Who'd have thought I'd someday share the same experience with my own children at this very same park.

I also remember my father trying to drive his new Chevrolet station wagon across the muddy road at the top of the levee dividing the two small lakes. He wound up getting stuck in a mud hole, and it took him a considerable amount of time before he was able to dislodge the car.

In his efforts to get out, he lowered the tailgate on the station wagon, and had my siblings and I sit on the tailgate to add weight to the back of the car. By the time we got unstuck, his shining white station wagon was covered in mud. Dad was fit to be tied. We, on the other hand, had fun bouncing up and down on the tailgate. For us it was a great adventure, and surely something he'd never let us repeat again.

Lastly, I remember swinging on a tire swing from a tall tree at the edge of the lake. These days, the tire swing is no longer there. But the tree was, as tall and majestic as I'd remembered it. Looking at it many years later brought a smile to my face.

I'd thought about this particular lake many times over the years, when I'd see the photographs we took in 1964, or see children playing on a tire swing, or drive by another lake somewhere else. I'd often wondered where it might be. And here it was, all along, just 36 miles from my hometown.

It dawned on me then that there are other places I pass by occasionally that give me the same eerie feeling of having been there at an earlier time. Now, whenever this happens, I make a point to stop and examine the site more closely. Occasionally, I will see something there that will jar something else in the far recesses of my mind, which in turn will cause old memories to come pouring out.

I firmly believe that pleasant memories of our childhoods are a big part of what makes life worth living. Beyond that, they give us something to do on those occasions when we're alone and lonely, and need something to warm our hearts.

I've been back to that lake several times since my discovery, even though I've had to go out of my way to do it. To others, it's just an ordinary lake in an ordinary park in a small town in Texas. But it's something special to me.

The Telescope

There was a time in my young life when I wanted more than anything else to be an astronaut. This coincided more or less with John Glenn's historic orbit around the earth, NASA's Mercury and Gemini programs, and the way the United States went "moon crazy" in the late 1960s and early 1970s.

I remember watching the "Eagle" land on the moon on my parents' old black and white RCA. It was an exciting time not only for me, but for every other young boy in the country as well.

I vividly recall going outside, gazing up at a brightly lit moon in the night sky, and feeling disappointed that I could not see the landing craft on the moon's surface.

Hey, I was only 11.

From that night on, I saw the moon in a different perspective. No longer just a gray ball of dirt in the sky, this body now had a form and a function. It was to be the home of a moon colony that I would someday inhabit. There was no doubt in my mind.

I had to get a closer look.

My friend Larry was an only child, and somewhat spoiled by his parents. He had a telescope in his bedroom that was capable of providing a close-up view of the lunar surface. The first night the moon was full after the moon landing, I was off to Larry's house to scan the moon's surface.

At first I was disappointed that I couldn't see the American flag the Apollo crew had left behind. Then, as I gazed more and more at the moon's surface, I became more and more impressed by its unspoiled beauty. I couldn't wait to get there.

I wanted my own telescope, so I could look at the moon from my own bedroom. Unfortunately, the old *Indian Chief Select* cigar box which held my life's savings contained only a few meager dollars. If I had to save for a telescope, it would take a whole summer's worth of mowing peoples' lawns. I couldn't wait that long.

Wesley "the Brain" offered a solution to my dilemma. He told me to invest in a dozen magnifying glasses. This made no sense to me, until he offered his logic to go along with the advice.

Wesley explained that one magnifying glass makes an object look five times larger than it actually is. A second magnifying glass, placed in front of the first, would make the object five *times* five times, or 25 times larger.

Confused? So was I, but Wesley was able to finally convince me that each time I added a magnifying glass to my homemade "telescope," my view of the moon would get five times better. He convinced me that eventually, my telescope would work better than Larry's, and I would even be able to see the flag.

I took a long cardboard tube and split it down the middle, so that I could glue the lenses on the inside of the tube. I carefully spaced the lenses two inches apart and set the contraption aside so that the glue could dry overnight.

That night I dreamed the dreams of a young boy longing for great adventure. I dreamed that through my telescope I could see creatures on other planets, including little green men on Mars, and three-headed dogs on the moon. I dreamed that NASA was so impressed by my discoveries that they let me head up the expeditions to meet with these creatures, and I became a national hero.

Hey, I was only eleven. In my world, anything was possible.

The next morning, I checked to see that the glue was dry, and then taped the tube closed again.

The moment of truth came when I took my creation outside, spotted a bird sitting on a telephone pole two houses away, and I hefted the telescope to my eye. I fully expected to count the feathers on the bird's neck. Instead, I saw… nothing.

Actually, that's not quite true. What I saw could best be described as a dark gray blob of nothingness. I was crushed.

Wesley looked through the telescope and then scratched his head. "I don't understand," he said. "It should work."

I lost a lot of faith in Wesley's thinking abilities that day. In fact, I think that's the day I stopped calling him "the Brain."

Wesley later came to me and said that he thought the problem was not enough light. The light, he said, got weaker each time it went through one of the lenses. I should poke holes in the tube between each lens, to allow more light in.

I asked him what good the holes would do at night, when I was going to be looking at the moon. He had no answer.

Needless to say, NASA never sent me on a moon mission. This was clearly Wesley's fault, and I never really forgave him for it.

Eventually, I stopped dreaming about going to the moon and lost most of my interest in things of an astrological nature. Perhaps I was slightly ahead of my time. Maybe my son or daughter, or one of my grandchildren, will have a chance to visit the Sea of Tranquility in my place.

I hope the three-headed moon dogs are still there.

A Dusty Old Attic

Every boy needs a place to hide his treasures.

Not just any place will do. It's got to be a place so secret that there is absolutely no chance that anyone will stumble across it. There should be a method of deterring others from even being in the area. Lastly, there must be a security system that will make it apparent any time an intruder has been around.

I suppose the ideal place would have been a locked vault, for which only I knew the combination, buried beneath ten feet of earth, with a motion-sensor alarm system and a sign over the spot reading "Stay out – land mines!"

Unfortunately, as much as I would have enjoyed playing with land mines, my resources as a small boy were somewhat limited. I therefore had to find a cheaper and lower tech way of securing my valuables.

Several times I buried shoe or cigar boxes in the back yard which contained things I considered important. Although this was a good way of hiding things, it had its drawbacks. For one, it was hard to protect my treasures from water damage, especially after a hard rain. Zip-lock bags didn't exist back then, and the fold-over sandwich bags didn't offer the same degree of protection.

Also, things buried for several weeks sometimes got hard to find again. There is a great scene in the movie "*Stand By Me*," that depicts a boy who spends weeks searching for a buried jar of change. I laugh out loud every time I watch that scene. I've been there, and I've done that. Once the grass grew over the spot where I buried things, it looked exactly like the rest of the yard. I sometimes had to dig several holes to find what I was looking for.

I finally gave up on planting things in the back yard after I lost a box full of Matchbox cars. I clearly remember planting them one spring to keep my little brother from playing with them, and then going back at the end of the summer to dig them back up again. Problem was, I couldn't remember the exact spot, and after digging twenty holes over a two-week period, I finally gave up.

My Matchbox cars are still there in the back yard of the house where I grew up. Somewhere.

After I lost my cars, I knew I had to find a better system of hiding my treasures. I finally found the perfect place when I was playing in the attic above my bedroom.

Actually, it wasn't an attic at all, but we called it that. It was actually a crawlspace in the rafters above the ceiling, full of itchy fiberglas insulation, dust and spiders. Lots and lots of spiders. That was the deterrence. Nobody in my family, not even my dad, would crawl up into the attic unless it was absolutely necessary. To do so would mean that on a good day they would get incredibly itchy and incredibly dirty. On a bad day they'd get bitten. It was enough to scare everyone off. Except me.

Into the attic, over the top of the ceiling toward the west end of the house, fourteen rafters from the trap door, under a thick piece of yellow insulation, was a large shoebox which held my most secret treasures.

Over the years, the contents of that box constantly changed. In my younger days, my autographed Don Drysdale baseball card was there, along with my favorite Hot Wheels cars, a few foreign coins I had collected, and several of my favorite comic books that I wanted to protect from my brother and sisters.

Later, the baseball cards and comics would be replaced by notes from teenage girls, passed across the classroom at school, a tattered copy of *Playboy* magazine, and literature about worldly places I wanted to visit someday. Also included was my first valentine from Danita Moore, a pilfered pack of Camel cigarettes and a book of matches, and a map of the state of Texas, for that day I was sure to come when I would run away from home.

My security system consisted of two small pieces of paper. I wedged one of them into the trap door of the attic every time I wiggled my way out of it. Virtually unnoticeable to anyone other than me, because I knew to look for it, the paper would have fluttered noiselessly to the ground any time the trap door was opened. By checking the trap door each evening, I would see the paper where I left it and know that no one had opened the door since I'd last checked.

A second piece of paper, no larger than a dime, was in the attic itself. It was atop the piece of insulation which covered my box, leaning up against the wooden support beam. Had anyone ever moved the insulation, I'd have noticed it immediately.

I never did take up smoking or run away from home (well, once, but I came back when I got hungry). Oddly enough, I don't remember ever bringing the box down. I think I finally grew up to the point where I just stopped checking on it.

Occasionally over the years I've wondered whether the box is still there, safely tucked away, slowly turning to dust. I've thought about going back to check on it several times, since my dad still owns that house.

That small house on 32nd Street has been sitting vacant for several years now. I'm sure the spiders took over the attic long ago. I suspect that's the real reason I don't want to go back. The spiders that once didn't bother me now give me chills. I'll settle for just enjoying my memories…

Apricot Pies

My Grandma Maloney used to make the most amazing fried apricot pies. They had no sugar, because she was a diabetic and had to strictly limit her sugar intake. But they were still the sweetest pies I've ever had.

Grandma lived in a small frame house just off of University Avenue, just a few blocks north of Texas Tech. I never really got to know my grandfather. He died when I was very young, so the only memories I have of him are vague and fuzzy. Grandma, on the other hand, lived to a ripe old age, passing on after I grew up and moved away.

We would periodically have supper at Grandma's house when I was a youngster. "Supper" to those not born and raised in west Texas, is typically called "dinner." "Dinner" to us was what non-Texans called "lunch."

Confused? It's simple, really. We had dinner at noontime and supper in the evening. Breakfast was called, well… "breakfast."

Anyway, back to Grandma's house and her fried pies. Grandma wasn't a bad cook. She made an excellent pot of beef stew or chicken and dumplings, and her baked chicken couldn't be beat.

Whatever she was serving that day, though, was really just a precursor to what we all really came for.

When my father and my uncles, and all of their wives and children finished eating, Grandma would chase all the men and kids out of the kitchen. The men would go into the living room, where they'd loosen their belts, take off their shoes, and relax on the overstuffed easy chairs. The women would hang around the kitchen, where they'd help clean up after the meal, do the dishes, and gossip. The kids would go down the stairs to the basement, which sat directly under the living room.

In the basement, we'd use an old, ragged ball to bounce off the wall, playing a game we'd invented that was very similar to handball. When we'd get tired of doing that, we'd read comic books or tell ghost stories or play with the toys that someone had brought over.

We knew it was getting close to pie time when we'd start hearing Grandma yelling at her sons to get their fingers out of her pies and get out of her kitchen.

The men, you see, had us at a disadvantage. While we could smell only the damp, dank basement, the smell of the baking pies would waft into the living room, where as if by magic it would pick my father and uncles up from their chairs and carry them toward the kitchen.

Once there, they would invariably try to snatch a taste of Grandma's pies. If successful, they kept snatching tastes until Grandma threw them out. If Grandma hadn't done so, there would have been nothing left for the children.

As I said before, Grandma's pies contained no sugar because she was a diabetic. Normally, any so-called "dessert" that contains no sugar earns upturned noses and disgust from an average kid. But these pies were different.

Maybe it was just because these pies came from our grandmother's experienced hands, but these pies were delicious.

Fried pies are made in individual-sized portions, with a hand-pressed crust a little smaller than a dinner plate. The filling is ladled generously in the center of the crust, which is then folded over, pressed along the edges, and fried in butter in a frying pan. Some people add a bit of sugar to the fruit filling, and coat the outer crust with a sugar glaze. Grandma did neither, yet her pies were the best I've ever eaten.

Years later, I talked my wife Barbara into trying this simple recipe. We didn't have an apricot tree in our back yard, as Grandma did, so we made a special trip to the grocery store to buy some. They were out of season, so we had to settle for the canned variety.

Barbara's effort was a dismal failure. Although there was absolutely nothing wrong with them, and they were promptly devoured by Barbara and the kids, they just weren't the same to me.

There are some things I will always remember my Grandma Maloney for. The kind smile on her face, the fact that I never heard her say an unkind word about anyone, the stern look she gave my father when he acted up that had the power of turning him from a mountain of a man into a chastised little boy.

But most of all, I remember how her aged hands and years of practice took a few simple ingredients and magically created a treat that still makes my mouth water, even after all these years…

A Boy's Best Friend

I've come to the conclusion that one of the most important things you can do for a child is to get them a pet of their own, to care for and protect, play with, and love. Those kids who have had pets around for their entire lives tend to take them for granted. Only those folks who grew up without such pleasures know what a big difference a pet can make in enriching a kid's life.

Just to set the record straight, I'm not talking about cats, hamsters, fish or birds. I'm talking about real pets. For a boy from my generation, the word pet was a synonym for "dog."

I'm no scientist, but I believe that if the world was divided between two types of young boys, those who had a dog and those who didn't, I think that the group who owned dogs would grow up to be far more successful, driven and happy. Just my opinion…

Anyway, I love my father tremendously. He is a caring, honest and giving man. But when I was growing up, he considered dogs a liability and expense, nothing more, and for that reason we were never able to talk him into getting us one.

Oh, we tried. Several times, we brought home strays, or puppies that a friend was giving away. Invariably, we wound up letting the strays go, and returning the puppies to their previous owners. Dad would say that dog food and vet bills were expensive, and that he couldn't afford to get sued if the dog bit one of our friends.

We tried to counter this argument by saying we'd find a friendly dog, who wouldn't eat much and would never ever bite anyone.

Dad always insisted that all dogs bite given the right circumstances, and we had trouble arguing the point. Twenty years of being a postman made Dad somewhat an expert on dog bites, having suffered them himself on a regular basis.

Perhaps the absence of a family pet was just a disadvantage of living in a large family on a limited income.

I never really accepted not having a dog of my own.

My little brother Randy and I once brought a German shepherd puppy home, named him Dusty, and hatched a plan to keep him and raise him secretly in our bedroom. We weren't very bright back then.

Randy and I pooled our change and had enough to buy him a few cans of dog food, laid down old newspapers in our bedroom closet, and visited the puppy periodically throughout the day to make sure he was okay.

About three in the morning on that first night, Dusty grew tired of whatever game these two humans appeared to be playing with him and decided that he wanted to play something else. He had gotten tired of sitting in the darkened closet awaiting our periodic visits.

He woke us up by softly whimpering, and got louder and louder, until we had to let him out of the closet and into our bedroom.

Thinking he'd be happy once he was out of the closet, we tried to go back to sleep when he decided he wanted to play. He began barking and running happily around the room, bumping into things in the dark and sliding around the smooth wooden floor.

This obviously would not do. I pulled him into bed with me and cupped my hand over his snout, while I lectured him in a loud whisper that it wasn't a good idea for him to bark in the middle of the night. Talking with the puppy in this manner, there was no doubt in my young and feeble mind, would solve the problem. Surely Dusty would understand every word I said, and would immediately comply with my request.

No sooner had I let go of Dusty's snout did he let out a loud bark, and start running around the bed. His tail wagged a thousand miles an hour, and he obviously interpreted my lecture as a sign that I wanted to play.

Randy, by this time, had his head buried under his pillow. I was sure he was trying desperately to appear to be asleep, so he'd be presumed innocent when our father came bursting into the room at any second.

I threw a blanket over Dusty in a last-ditch effort to silence him. This startled him, and he yelped a feeble cry, but he did stop barking. Then he relieved himself, flooding the center of my bed.

I had several choices. I could stay up all night with Dusty, petting and playing with him and trying my best to keep him quiet.

I could crawl out my bedroom window and put him in the back yard, where he'd surely start whimpering again.

I could sneak into my sisters' room across the hall, deposit him there, and then play stupid when my father found him and accused my sisters of harboring an unauthorized animal.

Although the third option had a kind of fiendish appeal, I knew that my dad would get rid of Dusty and I desperately wanted to keep him.

I stayed up all night with the puppy, thinking that the next night would certainly be better.

We spent the better part of our second day as pet owners taking Dusty on a tour of the neighborhood. He met all of our friends and got petted a million times. He ate cookies and remnants of baloney sandwiches and lots of dog biscuits. He had a blast. I had a hard time staying awake.

As the sky darkened that night, Randy went into the house and opened the bedroom window. I hefted Dusty up to my brother and he deposited the pup into his closet for what we hoped was the entire night.

It had been a very long and very tiring day for both of us. We were exhausted, and the prospect of having a puppy of our own was not as appealing as it once was. We hadn't known it would be this much work.

The second night was, of course, almost an exact copy of the first. Except that Dusty was kind enough to pee on the closet floor instead of my still-damp bed. He also left a surprise next to Randy's bed that Randy stepped in while getting out of bed.

By the end of the third night, we began to see Dusty as less of a faithful friend and more of a demon sent from the pits of hell to torment us for all eternity. Not really, but we were getting close.

We also had to figure out what to do with Dusty when school started a couple of weeks later, and we'd no longer be able to spend our days with him. Try as we might, that was a problem we had no solution for.

The fourth day, we took Dusty back to Mike's house and explained to his parents that our folks wouldn't let us keep him after all.

"Would you like for me to call your parents and try to talk them into it?" Mike's mom offered. We quickly declined her offer. As much as we appreciated her help, we knew Dad would blow his top when he found out we'd been covertly sheltering a pet in his home without permission.

Instead, we just gave up on having a dog at that particular time in our lives.

The first chance we could, we got dogs of our own, although that was sometime later. Today, as an adult, I just couldn't fathom a household without a family dog. In fact, I have even given into my wife and allowed the invasion of a couple of moody cats into our humble abode. This is despite my lifelong belief that cats are only good for throwing shoes at.

All of my adult children have dogs of their own. Hopefully, none of my grandchildren will ever have to resort to hiding animals in their bedroom closets.

A post-script to this story:

My dad eventually got over his dislike of dogs. Shortly after his last child grew up and moved out, he developed an affection for black Labrador retrievers. Perhaps the house was just too quiet for him. Maybe he met someone who had a black lab and was impressed with its loyalty and affection.

We don't know for sure what the reason was. What we do know is that for many years now he has had a series of black labs. He always names them Sparky, regardless of their gender, because he says he's too old to remember a new name for each new dog. He always adopts them from the local dog pound, and I understand that he gets a call from the pound every time a stray black lab comes in to see if he's ready for the next one.

We've lost track of whether his current dog is Sparky number 6 or Sparky number 7. Whichever it is, we're just glad that Dad, in his golden years, has finally realized the joy that a good dog can bring into a life. That's something we knew even way back then.

Lawn Food

Most boys have some rather odd habits when they're growing up. Some stick their tongue out of the corner of their mouth when they're reading or concentrating. Some absent-mindedly pick their noses, or scratch their heads when they're puzzled by something, or scratch other parts of their bodies without thinking. Take an adolescent boy and watch him long enough, and you're bound to stumble across at least one peculiar habit.

Actually, I had several annoying habits when I was a kid. One of the oddest, which I actually carried into adulthood, was eating plants and flowers.

Not just any plants and flowers, mind you. I spent many years developing a taste for particular types of flower blossoms, and eventually I became a connoisseur. I knew which petals were too bitter to eat, which ones had a delicate sweet taste, and which had no taste at all.

It's been far too many years to remember how this particular trait started out. If I were a betting man, though, I'd bet that I probably did it for the first time to annoy some of the girls in the neighborhood.

These days, there is a term that boys use when they want to do something so disgusting that they turn up their noses, scream "eeewww!!!" and run off to tell their friends what little Billy did. The term today is "gross out," as in "Billy, here comes Sarah. Pick your nose and gross her out."

Back then, we didn't have a term to describe those adolescent acts of crudeness, but the intent was the same. So was the effect. I probably ate a fistful of flowers for the first time to encourage a pesky girl to run off and tattle to her friends.

Actually, flower petals aren't bad at all, if you eat the right ones. My Grandma Maloney lived for a long time on Colgate Street in my hometown in Texas. We'd visit her each Sunday after church.

I wish I had a nickel for every time Grandma chased me out of her flower beds. She had an assortment of flowers that grew each spring adjacent to her front porch. When she wasn't looking, I'd pick the petals off the small red flowers that made up the bulk of her flower collection. The red ones were just the right flavor to make them enjoyable. The white flowers, on the other hand, were downright nasty.

I learned sometime later that some flower petals can temporarily dye your mouth and lips the same color. Fortunately, the little red flowers at Grandma's house didn't do that, or my goose would have been cooked every time.

As the girls got older, they started to change. When a girl is six, watching a boy eat flowers is just crazy enough to be scary.

Ten years later, though, the same girl is sixteen and finds it funny that a boy of equal age is willing to do such a stunt. A sixteen year old boy has learned that eating flowers, then making a funny face, is a good way to make a girl of his affection laugh. He has also learned by this time that laughter is one of the ways to a girl's heart.

Of course, my wife thinks she's the only one I ever ate flowers for. Let's not tell her otherwise.

I didn't stop at flower petals. I used to collect sour clover by the handful when I was a young teenager living in San Antonio. It would grow wild in our back yard in the spring and early summer, and I would gather it up and chew on the stems. They had a taste to them that was decidedly sour, yet tart at the same time, almost like a green apple.

Before long, I had all of my friends chomping on clover like livestock. Adults all over the neighborhood thought we were insane. They didn't know what they were missing.

Any good gardener knows that there is nothing in this world better than raw green beans or black-eyed peas, picked fresh off the vine. The same thing holds true for cucumbers when they are about as long as your thumb.

Granted, all of these things are acquired tastes, and I have never tried to make a meal out of any of them. Their nutritional value is probably on the low end of the scale.

Still, for entertainment value, grabbing a handful of flowers in front of a girl you're trying to impress, chomping down the petals, and handing her the stems, is guaranteed to get a laugh from her. It's better than telling her you're willing to swim the world's oceans for her, then jumping fully clothed into a fountain. I've done that too, and darned near caught pneumonia. But that's a story for another time…

Where Did All The Good Music Go?

My children and grandchildren laugh at me when I tell them that there hasn't been any good music since Credence Clearwater Revival and Steppenwolf. Then they ask who these bands were. I used to laugh at Pat Boone and Bill Haley and the Comets when I was their age. To me, 1950s music was more "old and moldy" than "golden oldies."

My kids don't believe it now, but their children will someday make fun of their generation's choice of music. It's a rite of passage that's been around as long as the phonograph record, and maybe even before that.

When I was a youngster, my house was filled with the music of Ray Price, Faron Young, and the Sons of the Pioneers. To my father, no other music existed. It wasn't until my oldest sister, Glenda, started bringing home records by the Beatles and Strawberry Alarm Clock, that we even had another type of music available. Even then, we only heard it when Dad was at work.

Back then, my father started his decades-long habit of collecting old records. Here's how to tell if someone is *really* old: ask them what a "78" is. Most people younger than 60 will guess that it's the year that came after '77.

A "78" is an old term for a 78 RPM record from the golden age of music. They started going out of style in the 1950s, and by the early 1960s, they weren't being manufactured at all.

Slightly smaller than the 33 RPM record "album," but larger than the 45 RPM single, the 78 usually came in a plain brown wrapper with a donut-sized hole in the middle. The hole was there so you could read the record label.

At one time, my father's old record collection was so extensive that he devoted one room of the house just for storing the things. He sorted them by recording company first: Liberty Records, Columbia Records, the Decca label. Then they were sorted by artists' names: Gene Autry, Don Gibson, Hank Snow, Ernest Tubbs…

He bought several shelving units from a record store that was moving across town and no longer needed them. Once they were full, he started creating tall stacks of records on every square inch of floor space. It eventually became hard to walk around the room. The records were everywhere.

Dad used to drive to area towns on the weekends and visit record shops to add to his collection, and occasionally traded records with friends. It wasn't just a hobby, he said, it was a source of extra income. He did sell some occasionally, and he probably made a modest profit on his sales. The problem was, he had a hard time parting with most of the albums, and for every one he sold he bought 10 more.

When dad worked outside in those days, he'd take a portable phonograph player and put it on the porch. Then he'd crank it up, and would pull weeds, or push his wheelbarrow, or repair the fence, or whatever, with Hank Williams Sr.'s voice wafting around the neighborhood. In a way, my dad's portable record player was the grandfather of the boom box.

Of course, the neighbors probably didn't appreciate the loud music invading their airspace. Oddly enough, though, I don't remember any of them ever complaining about it. It may be because back then there was a limited choice of music. Rock and roll was in its infancy, and hadn't yet caught on in our very conservative neighborhood. Big band music had run its course and was in its waning years of popularity. In essence, my dad's music was what pretty much everyone in the neighborhood listened to, and they could relate to it. So maybe they just enjoyed the free entertainment.

I hope that's what it was. Either that or they considered my father insane and thought it best to just stay away from him. I suppose I'll never know for sure.

When 78s stopped being produced, record players began being made without an option for that particular speed. I remember that in the 1960s, Dad started buying and stockpiling older record players, so that he'd always be able to hear his 78s. When asked why he just didn't switch to 33s and 45s like everyone else in the free world, he said that the record companies didn't appreciate good music and that 33s were a "load of garbage." In other words, his preferred taste for music was going out of style along with the 78, and he didn't like the newer styles of music everyone else was going to.

In the 1960s, my friends and I seldom had time to listen to the radio. We were very seldom near one, since we spent practically every waking hour outside in the fresh air, playing sports or riding our bikes or getting into mischief. Listening to the radio was one of those things we did only on rainy days, when none of our friends were available to come over, and there was nothing else to do.

Because of this, and because Glenda could only play her music on those rare occasions when mom and dad were both gone, that the music of the 1960s pretty much passed me by. It wasn't until my high school years that I began to appreciate the "good old rock and roll" from the previous decade. Then, Sam Baker and I would ride around in his old green Ford Pinto and listen to 8-track tapes of rock and roll from the Woodstock era.

When the 8-track went the way of the old 78s, I could relate to the way my father must have felt twenty years earlier. I swore that the cassette tape would fail, because at that time it lacked what was the best feature or the 8-track tape: continuous play.

An 8-track tape, for you youngsters, would play in a continuous loop, repeating the songs over and over again until you turned it off. Early cassette tape players, on the other hand, did not have "auto reverse." That came later on. This meant that in those years, you'd have to listen to the five or six songs on side "A," then eject the tape and flip it over, and reinsert it to hear side "B." It was decidedly inconvenient, especially when you were in the back seat of your car trying to make out with your best girl.

For that reason, I thought the cassette tape was just a temporary thing. I thought that the industry would get so many complaints about the new cassettes, that they would abandon them and go back to making 8-tracks.

I was wrong. In their never-ending quest for anything newer, smaller, better, America's consumers chose the cassette over 8-tracks, and 8-tracks were no longer produced after the late 1970s. It was the end of an era. I seriously considered stocking up on 8-track tapes and players.

It was shortly after that, when he 1980s came rolling in, that rock music became deafening, and the words were no longer written with feeling. That was okay, though, because the guitars were so loud they drowned out the words anyway.

It was during his period in my life that I developed a real taste for (don't laugh) country music. Back then it was called "country and western," and a new breed of performers was looming on the horizon to not only shorten its name, but to bring it an international prestige it had never had before. Country music was in. Seemingly, based on today's multi-billion dollar country music industry, it's in to stay.

I was listening to a country station not long ago on my way back from Dallas, and heard the Sons of the Pioneers sing "Cool Water." I hadn't heard the song in decades, and it instantly took me back to my childhood. As I listened to the harmony of this group of long-dead crooners, I found that its peaceful melody relaxed me and took me back to simpler times. I think I finally understood what my father saw in this kind of music and it made me realize that maybe I'm not so different than him after all.

Fireworks

Watch a man, any man, the next time you sit near him at an action movie. When Mel Gibson narrowly misses getting himself blown to pieces by a massive explosion, the man's eyes will get bigger, his mouth will start to water, and he'll wish that he could have been the one to press the plunger on the explosive charge.

Sure, the movie is okay. Lots of action and adventure, and even a little bit of (yuck) romance. But what really attracts an average man to movies of this type (besides the beautiful actress playing opposite Gibson) is the chance to watch things get blown up. That's part of the little boy inside of every man... the part of him that never grew up.

It starts early. About the time a typical boy turns nine or ten, his parents finally trust him to start lighting his own firecrackers. Lay it on the ground, they tell him, then light it and quickly run away.

The little boy rolls his eyes, follows the instructions, and puts his parents' minds at ease. They are pleased to see that he is responsible, can handle fireworks safely, and will never be hurt by misusing these pint-sized explosives.

There are a couple of things the parents don't know, of course. One is that their son has been playing with firecrackers for years with his friends. Another is that he *has* been hurt by waiting too long to throw a firecracker, or by picking up what he thought was a "dud" only to find out it was a slow-burner instead. They don't have to tell him that firecrackers hurt like the dickens when they blow up in your hand, and that they make your fingers numb for hours. He'd already found out this stuff the hard way.

My little brother Randy and I started as most boys do, by merely lighting the firecrackers and throwing them. Unfortunately, this will entertain boys for only so long, before they need something bigger, better, flashier.

We graduated next to tying the firecrackers together into a bundle of three or four, then twisting their fuses together.

By lighting the entwined fuses, they went off more or less at the same time, and presto... we tripled or quadrupled our firepower instantly.

We'd lay these bundles of firecrackers on the ground, put a empty tin can over the top of them with one edge of the can's open end resting on the firecrackers. Then we'd light them and try to blow the can over the house. We succeeded a couple of times, but most often it fell short and came tumbling down the roof back to us.

For my sisters in the house, it drove them crazy... "pow, clunk, rattle, rattle, rattle" over and over again. Not that driving my sisters crazy was something I ever really worried about.

To annoy the neighbors, we sometimes got up at 6 a.m. on a Saturday and tossed one of those bundles into an empty garbage can outside someone's bedroom window. I know you young whippersnappers don't remember this, but garbage cans used to be made of galvanized steel. They were heavy, lasted forever, and amplified the sound of four small firecrackers so that they sounded like cannon going off. It was loud enough to wake the dead. Or at least a grouchy neighbor from a sound sleep.

No wonder we weren't very popular with the older folks around the neighborhood.

Somewhere along the line, we started blowing up red ant beds. These huge creatures were a constant source of irritation to my friends and I. We'd all been bitten numerous times while playing football, or just laying around in the grass watching the clouds go by and talking about important stuff like baseball and aliens.

We'd exact our revenge by screwing a firecracker into the entrance of their tunnel. The ants would swarm all over the firecracker, trying to figure out what it was and whether it was edible.

We'd sit back and wait until the ants completely covered the firecracker. Only then would we light the fuse.

Of course, this particular stunt also had its hazards for us. While most of the ants were instantly blown to bits, there was an occasional lucky beast who was merely blown intact through the air. Occasionally one of the lucky guys would land on us, where he would exact his own revenge. I was stung on the lower lip once, and the entire bottom of my face swelled up like an inner tube. It wasn't a pretty sight.

From time to time, we'd hang Larry's model airplanes from a tree branch with a piece of fishing line, so that they hung freely beneath the branch. Then we'd tie a *Black Cat* (the firecracker of choice in my crowd) to their wings, and blow them to smithereens.

Then we'd pick up the smithereens up and throw them al into a shoebox. The next rainy day, we'd glue the pieces together again so we could repeat the process later.

We all dreamed of being Navy Seals some day, blowing up warships and real airplanes. No doubt many of us full-grown men, given a chance, would still take such a job, as long as we could do it without having to exercise.

Blowing stuff up, or wanting to, is just something guys never outgrow.

Gone Fishing

I can't explain it. In the same way ice cream tastes better if you make it yourself, even though the ingredients are the same as those in the store-bought variety, fishing is always more fun when you skip school to do it. I know it sounds illogical, but it's a fact of life. Just ask any boy.

Cutting school was a hazardous proposition when I was in fourth grade, even more so for me personally than it was for my friends. Since my sister Karen was two grades ahead of me, and my twin sister Debbie was in the classroom next to mine, there were simply too many Maloney kids running around P.F. Brown Elementary School on any given day. This increased the chances that the attendance monitor would bump into one of my sisters in the hall and ask them if I was feeling poorly, since I hadn't come to school that day.

My sisters, you see, couldn't be trusted to keep their mouths closed. Not one of them. If they had even the slightest hint that I had skipped school, or did anything else I wasn't supposed to do, they'd race each other home at the end of the school day and sing like a pair of canaries.

Danny and Ronnie didn't have the same problem. Their sisters didn't care if they showed up at school or not. Kent and Larry and Wesley didn't have any siblings that attended our school. So it was a bit easier for them, on that warm spring morning, when we were sitting outside the school waiting for the opening bell to ring, and discussing how we hadn't been fishing for awhile.

"We oughta just play hooky," Kent suggested. "I'm tired of school anyway."

That's all the convincing it took. Ten minutes later we were on the earthen levee that separated the two lakes at Clapp Park, four blocks south of the school. The only tree on the levee, a medium-sized willow, offered low hanging branches that provided protection from prying eyes as well as the afternoon sun.

I remember covertly traveling the distance to Clapp Park, sneaking down alleyways and peeking around corners. None of us had ever seen a truant officer, but we knew they were out there, lurking, waiting to pounce on us if we spent too much time in one spot.

We sent Wesley home to get his fishing gear and a couple of rods, since he lived closest to the lake and because both of his parents worked during the day. When he returned he had his tackle box, two rods and reels from his garage, and a package of Oreo cookies he'd had hidden under his bed. We already had some worms we dug up while waiting for Wesley to come back, so we were all set.

For the rest of that morning, we sat in the shadows of that willow with our fishing lines in the water. We really didn't expect to catch anything, but it still beat the heck out of sitting in a classroom. We ate our lunches when the sun was high in the sky and whiled our day away.

We used to refer to Wesley as the brain of our group, because over the years he'd come up with some really great ideas for gags and pranks. But Wesley could also be a bit on the dim side sometimes, and occasionally he'd pull a prank that we would all pay a heavy price for.

We talked about the field trip we'd taken to the Garden and Arts Center the week before. Among the art they had on display were several prize-winning posters from the high school's anti-drug campaign.

Back then, the drug of choice among hippies and draft dodgers was something called LSD. We didn't know what it was, nor did we care. We were just innocent little kids. So the poster we saw on display that depicted a scary skull saying "LSD: It'll Ruin Your Life" didn't have that much significance to us. It looked cool, but that's about it.

However, before we left the facility a mere hour later, that same poster had become something of a firestorm of controversy. At some point during that hour, one of the miscreants in our class had taken a Bic pen and added a few letters to the poster. It now read "Lubbock School District: It'll Ruin Your Life."

The incident caused much embarrassment to the teachers who accompanied us on the field trip, and the principal at our school had been looking high and low for the culprit. We hadn't known it was Wesley until he nonchalantly confessed his crime at the lake that afternoon.

Our first thought was to gang up on Wesley and pummel him into the dirt. He was the cause of each of us being dragged into Mr. Autry's office the day after the field trip. One at a time, Principal Autry tied us to s chair and stomped around us with his Nazi jackboots, hitting his riding crop repeatedly into his left hand and demanding that we come clean or face a firing squad. The heat from the klieg lights shining brightly in our eyes made us sweat, but none of us cracked.

Okay, maybe that's a slight exaggeration, but we were interrogated and it wasn't much fun.

But we couldn't really be mad at Wesley for the prank. We all thought it was funny, and if anything we were each jealous that we hadn't thought of it first.

This led to a discussion about exactly what drugs were and how they made people act, which led to Wesley leaving the sanctuary of the tree branches and stumble awkwardly around the levy like a drunken fool. That, in turn, caught the eye of a passing motorist, who happened to be a police officer in a marked patrol car.

The policeman promptly pulled over, stepped out of his car, and yelled at us from across the lake.

He said we'd better be back in school the next time he drove by. Wesley sheepishly yelled back "yes, sir." The cop climbed back into his car, went on his way, and we sat down to discuss our new dilemma.

The cop didn't say when he was coming back. Should we go back to school, get paddled, and have to carry notes home to our parents? Or should we wait half an hour until school was over, taking the chance that the policeman would come back in the interim and catch us still at the lake?

Wesley had gotten us into this mess, and it was only fair that he should get us out of it.

"Let's go to school," he said, "but we'll take the long way around the lake. Then we'll walk real slow, and make sure we don't get back to school before everybody gets out. If the cop comes back, he'll see we're heading toward the school and he'll leave us alone."

We stashed the fishing gear in a drainage culvert for Wesley to retrieve on his way home and walked those four blocks at a snail's pace. The dismissal bell rang when we were crossing the street to the campus. I met my sisters at the usual place and we walked home together. They hadn't had a clue that I wasn't in school all day.

After supper, the five of us met again at Mark's house, and we all forged notes from each other's dads excusing us from being "ill" that day. We'd learned long before that our novice handwriting wouldn't pass muster as our mothers' writing. But it was good enough to pass for our dads'.

And, like all boys of that age, we took great pride that we'd gotten away with our day away from school. So much so that we did it several more times over the next couple of years.

Stee-Rike Three!

These days I consider myself a pretty good softball player. This more or less comes with the territory when you've raised three boys, since you tend to get lots of practice. As a youngster, though, I was no better than average. Nothing wrong with that, except that sometimes it hurt when I failed myself and my teammates.

Two things can be said about kids that are almost universal in nature. The first is that kids can be really cruel. They don't necessarily mean to be, it's just because they lack the social training that comes later in life.

In the absence of good graces, they say things not knowing or caring how they sound to the recipient.

The other thing that is universal about kids is that they will cut each other absolutely no slack when an important game is on the line.

For these reasons, it's not surprising that most men who played sports as a kid can remember as though it were yesterday the time they struck out in the big game. Or the time they missed a game-winning three pointer with half a second left on the cloak. Or the time they missed an easy tackle and gave up the winning touchdown. These memories tend to stay with us forever.

As I said, my talents when I played little league at Clapp Park left much to be desired. Still, like most kids that age, I wanted to play baseball, so I talked my dad into signing me up. I remember how good it felt the first time I put on that red jersey with the number 5 on the back. "Kelly Tile and Supply," our team's sponsor, was emblazoned on the front. I was the king of the world.

I became very familiar with the bench. Our coach considered me and several of my teammates "slackers," who did the team more good when we weren't in the game. I think this was partly due to our lack of observable talent, and partly because we didn't "hustle" at practice as much as he wanted us to. In any event, we "slackers" sat on the bench during most of the games and killed time by yelling at the opposing team's batters, and watching the people in the bleachers.

This all changed one warm day about halfway through the season. Boy Scout Troop 111 took all of their Webelos on an overnight camping trip, and this left our team a bit short on players for our game that evening. The coaches had no choice but to let some of the slackers into the game.

The other team's pitcher was having an off day. He had already walked several of the batters the previous inning, and my teammate ahead of me in the batting order took his base on four straight balls.

The coach gave me some tender fatherly advice before I trotted off to the plate: "Don't you dare do anything stupid, like swing at the ball. Just stand there like a dummy and he'll walk you."

For the first pitch, I followed the coach's instructions to the letter, and the ball whizzed right past me. Directly over the plate, but too low. Ball one.

The next pitch was a bit outside, and again too low. But it was hittable, and it made me think about disregarding the instructions the coach had given me and knocking the next one out of the park.

I was convinced I could do it, but never got the chance. The third pitch hit me on the left side, right below my ribcage, and I was off to first base.

On my way to the base, I passed the dugout and heard the only civil words Coach Bannon ever said to me: "Way to take a hit, kid!"

The pitcher was replaced, and our side was put out without me ever feeling the pleasure of crossing home plate.

In the ninth inning, I was back in the batter's box, the target of a considerably better pitcher. I had a called strike against me as well as a ball. I decided that it was now or never. I was either going to knock the stuffing out of the ball or go down in flames.

The third pitch was right over the plate, and I got a piece of it. It popped high, and fouled over my team's dugout. Strike two.

I glanced over at the coach. He was eyeing me nervously, knowing that I was going to take the swing but not having the guts to tell me to let it go for fear it would be a called strike and make him look like an idiot. So he said nothing.

In my mind's eye I can still see the pitcher release the ball as though it were yesterday. It floated gracefully toward me, a bit higher than it should have been, and then dropped slightly just in front of the plate.

I swung my Louisville Slugger with everything I had, expecting a loud "whack" and a stinging sensation as the vibrations ran through my fingers. Instead, I heard the most awful sound in the world to a batter with two strikes against him... the "whoosh" of a bat hitting nothing but air. Strike three.

"Way to go, stupid," offered the son of one of the coaches when I returned to the dugout. Another was even less subtle. "No wonder the coach never lets you play." The words stung then, and still do today.

We had another out to go. The player after me singled to right field, and the next knocked a lazy pop fly ball right to the shortstop. The game was over and we lost by three runs.

I knew in my heart that I wasn't the only one who made mistakes in that game, and I wasn't the only one who struck out. But had I gotten a base hit, we'd have had two runners on and an extra out to play with, and who knows what might have happened.

Funny how a little thing like a baseball game can haunt you for half a lifetime...

The Ballpark

It didn't take me long to discover as a youngster that I wasn't any good at little league baseball. In the decades since my last little league game, I've raised three sons who have all played ball at one time or another, and I've gotten much better myself by working with them. As a twelve year old, though, my abilities as a ball player were woefully inadequate.

I guess it's not surprising, then, that my little league career only lasted two seasons. I only played in a handful of games, seldom got a base hit, and usually only made it as far as first base thanks to poor pitchers who either walked me or struck me with a pitch.

Oh, I still spent plenty of time at the ballpark. My friends and I discovered that there are many things to do at a little league ballpark that are at least as much fun as playing in the game.

During the seasons I played, I remember watching my friends Mark and Wesley hanging around the dugouts, hoping to catch a foul ball. A foul ball was worth a snow cone or a small coke if you turned it into the concession stand. For kids with little money to spend, this could mean the difference between having a cold refreshing drink or going thirsty. That probably explained why my friends got the majority of the baseballs sailing out of the park. Their thirst gave them a bit of incentive that kids with change in their pockets didn't have.

The thrid season I chose not to sign up for baseball, and opted instead to join my friends off the field. Wesley, Mark and I would shag the balls behind each of the dugouts and home run balls hit over the left field fence. The home run balls were of even more value, since proud fathers would often pay a couple of bucks for the ball their son hit out of the park.

Sometimes my little brother Randy and my friend Dennis would join us and we'd spend several hours at the Clapp Park ball fields, until all of the games were done for that day.

There were other boys out there shagging balls with us too. Most of them kept the balls and took them home with them. For my friends and me, we didn't have much need for them. In our neighborhood, football was the sport of choice. We spent much of our free time playing flag football in our front yards, or playing basketball at one of the local parks. We seldom played baseball, which probably explains why I wasn't much good at it. I was much better at football.

Besides us and the other foul chasers, there were a group of little brothers, who were too young to join the team. Lacking the attention of mom and dad, who had their eyes glued to the game, these little guys ran rampant throughout the bleachers stepping on toes and getting into mischief. We frequently used the guys to pull pranks on our friends and on spectators we didn't know.

Collectively, we were the "bleacher bunch," and I imagine we were every bit as entertaining as some of the slower games.

We won our nickname one evening when a couple of the little brothers sat several rows behind home plate and began throwing ice cubes at the plate umpire. After the first couple went sailing past his head, he called time, turned around, and eyed the crowd suspiciously. Of course, the miscreants were behaving like angels then. My friends and I were sitting next to the boys trying our best to control our laughter.

A couple of minutes later, a chunk of ice hit the ump in the back of the neck. Outraged, he whirled around, threw a thumb in the general direction of where the ice came from, and yelled to the home team coach "You better get that bleacher bunch to behave themselves or I'm calling the game!"

The coach threw up both hands and gave the umpire a puzzled look. You could almost read his mind as he thought "I can't even control this bunch of hoodlums in my dugout, and you want me to watch the fans too?"

He didn't say that, but I'm sure it's what he was thinking. Instead, he made a halfhearted attempt to walk over to the stands, give a stern look to several boys who may or may not have been the culprits, and then go back to his dugout.

From that day on, we called ourselves the "bleacher bunch" any time we were at the ballpark.

When we weren't chasing baseballs, we'd hang out at the concession stand trying to talk the vendor out of a free hot dog for sweeping out the stand or picking up the litter outside. He was responsible for cleaning the park after the last game, and we knew that many nights he'd be too tired to do so. So he'd frequently trade us something to eat or a snow cone each for doing it for him. We figured hey, we were there anyway, so why not? Besides, it was a great way to find lost change.

Other times we'd hang out under the bleachers looking for nickels and dimes that got fell out of the spectators' pockets. Or we'd sit on the top row of seats and shoot spit wads or pour water on the kids walking down the sidewalk below.

More than once, the park manager asked us to go home.

Things haven't changed much in the years since I spent my evenings at that ball field. When my youngest son Justin played his last year of little league in Alamogordo, New Mexico a few years ago, the kids were there, shagging foul balls in exchange for free bottles of Gatorade. They still raised a ruckus in the bleachers by dreaming up new pranks to occupy their time.

I suppose the bleacher bunch is a tradition as old as baseball itself. I have a brand new grandson named Mason, and another one named R.J. who will be here in a few weeks.

I'll do the same thing with my grandsons that I did with my sons. I'll try to spark an interest in baseball, and if it takes, I'll be there to watch their games. When I'm sitting in a bleacher twelve years from now watching one of them pitch their first no-hitter, I'll probably have a couple of spit wads stuck in my hair courtesy of some youngster high above me in the stands.

The Golden Horseshoe Drive-In

America lost something of great value when, a generation ago, it started shutting down its drive-in movie theaters. One by one these once-thriving establishments closed their gates, dismantled their mammoth screens, and went out of business. The first ones to fall were the victims of greedy real estate speculators who convinced the owners that their thirty acres of land were worth much more as a shopping mall.

Ironically, these same malls housed the mega-theaters that hastened the demise of the remainder of the drive-ins. The drive-ins simply couldn't compete against air conditioned multi-screen theaters that could operate year around and not be at the mercy of the weather. The multiplex offered a selection of ten movies to choose from, as opposed to one or two at the drive-in.

I was about six the first time my parents took my siblings and I to a drive-in movie. I've long ago forgotten the name of that first movie, and I suppose it doesn't really matter. The mere pleasure of the experience was more fun, at least to me, than was the movie itself.

Back then, the Golden Horseshoe Drive-In sat on University Avenue in my hometown of Lubbock, Texas. The Horseshoe had two monstrous movie screens on opposite ends of a huge lot, surrounded by a twelve-foot fence. For a large family looking for reasonably-priced entertainment on a summer night, this was the place to be.

Lubbock was known back then as a "church town," because the number of churches per capita far exceeded the national average. It was said that the churches' influence caused Lubbock to be declared "dry," and forced residents to drive outside the city limits to buy liquor or beer.

The number of churches in Lubbock during the early 1960s is relevant only because they were bad for business for the drive-in theater. Since all of the Protestant churches offered Wednesday night services at 7:30 p.m., about the same time drive-ins usually start their first viewing, most city residents were sitting in pews listening to their ministers instead of sitting in their cars listening to John Wayne or Jimmy Cagney. Hence, that night was a guaranteed bust for the drive-ins. Most of them didn't even bother opening on Wednesdays.

The Golden Horseshoe tried to counter these losses by offering a "carload" price on Friday nights. Drivers paid one price, three dollars, regardless of the number of people they had in their cars.

This was great for high school kids, who were on limited budgets and could pool their change, cram ten persons into an automobile, and drive through the Horseshoe gate, carefully avoiding potholes so they didn't leave their low-hanging bumpers behind.

There were also several times in our high school years when we had so many kids who wanted to go, and so little money to spare, that we locked a couple of friends in the trunk. Sometimes we'd even let them out in time to catch the end of the movie.

The carload price was also ideal for large families like mine, who enjoyed going out but whose entertainment budget was practically nonexistent.

We'd drive to the theater about a half hour before sunset and pick a good spot several rows back from the screen, and preferably directly in front of it. Dad would drive up to the speaker stand, pull it into the car, and try it out.

All of the speakers had a certain amount of static, but some were much worse than others. If Dad didn't like the first speaker, he'd put it back on the stand and drive forward to the next row to try again. Sometimes he'd do this three or four times, and it was great fun for us youngsters. Each row of speaker stands, you see, was elevated on a huge mound of earth, so that the front of the car pointed upward toward the movie screen. Driving over these mounds was somewhat akin to taking a short roller coaster ride.

If that last sentence sounds ridiculous, you've never been to Lubbock. The Lubbock area is flatter than a pancake, and hills pretty much don't exist unless they're man-made.

Mountains in the Lubbock area don't exist at all. So, yes. Driving over a mound of dirt counts as entertainment for kids under 10.

Once Dad found a speaker that met his standards, he'd turn off the car, turn off his lights, and tell us to go play until we got hungry for popcorn. We'd run off to the playground, which consisted of a slide and a swing set directly in front of the screen, and play until the cartoons started. Then we'd wander back to our car, looking at the high school kids who were too busy making out to watch the cartoons, which was okay because they obviously hadn't come to watch them anyway.

Back in the car, we'd watch the short cartoons that always preceded the first movie, and then the pitch to visit the refreshment stand for snacks. Dancing boxes of popcorn and drinks with legs and smiling faces would dance across the screen trying to entice customers to buy goodies. "Three minutes till show time," a talking bag of potato chips would say. "Better hurry!"

We once stayed at the playground and watched the cartoons and refreshment stand commercials from directly beneath the screens. The cartoons were cool, but there was something creepy about a forty-foot tall box of popcorn dancing above your head that gave my little brother nightmares for weeks. He kept waking up in the middle of the night thinking the popcorn was going to grab him and pop his head. We only did that once.

If the movie was boring, we'd walk over to the snack bar and hang out there, playing with old friends or making new ones. On hot nights, the cool metal seats outside the snack bar were far more comfortable than the car, because there was generally a soft breeze to cool us off. If we were lucky enough to have some spare change in our pocket, we'd buy a large coke for twenty cents and share it while we played.

On cool nights, we'd lay down on a mattress that Dad would put in the back of the station wagon for us, and crawl under a blanket to watch the movie. More often than not, we'd fall asleep during the movie and would be jostled awake when we returned home later.

The Golden Horseshoe closed years ago, replaced by a Super K-Mart. It was the first drive-in theater in town to close, and was followed closely thereafter by the Red Raider and Corral. In my mind, that's a rotten shame. I have absolutely nothing against K-Mart, but the theater was so much more fun. And in my memory it still is.

The Crawl Space

All little boys need a private place where they can go to be alone with their inner thoughts, plan their future, sulk, and plot revenge against their enemies. If they do not have such a place, they grow sullen, moody, and, well, act like little girls.

Eventually these boys turn into men, and the need changes. Actually, the need is still there, it just manifests itself in a different way. Instead of needing a quiet place to be alone in our thoughts, we require a soft couch and a football game where we can filter out everything going on around us. It serves the same basic need.

I say this only half jokingly. I grew up as one of five children. Our family was crammed into a modest three bedroom home. There wasn't a great opportunity for solitude within these confines, so I had to look elsewhere.

Many times in my youth I spent my quiet time atop the garage, hidden by a thick blanket of branches from an ancient elm tree. I played with the neighbor's cat, who hung out in the tree and always jumped down to the roof to greet me when I came to visit.

When the days were hot and still, and the rooftop was unbearable, I had the cool, dark recesses of the crawlspace beneath my parents' house.

In the center of the floor in our bedroom closet, set in the creaky boards of a maple wood floor, was a trap door about 24 inches square. I had seen my dad crawling in and out of the door several times when he was dismantling the old floor furnace right after we moved into the house in 1962. My curiosity was piqued, and I knew that eventually I'd have to sneak down there and do some exploring.

Every boy has an adventurous side. They say that curiosity killed the cat. It also landed many a young boy in situations he had no business being in. But that's part of growing up, and there aren't many men who won't confess to going exploring in forbidden places in their youth.

The crawl space beneath the house was strictly off-limits, according to my dad. So was the "attic," which wasn't really an attic at all, but merely another crawlspace above the ceiling.

Of course, placing such areas off-limits to boys simply makes them want to explore them more.

The first time I pried open that trap door with a screwdriver, I just knew for certain I was going to get caught. I was probably about seven, and the prospect of my father reaching down into the chasm and pulling me back up by the scruff of my neck was enough to send shivers up my spine. But not enough to keep me from proceeding through the hole.

I remember that it was a rainy day, and I was trapped indoors with nothing to do. Randy and I were laying on our beds trying to dream up an adventure. I don't remember whose idea it was to open up the trap door, but I very distinctly recall Randy being the one who rushed off to find a screwdriver. Therefore, I can honestly say it was partly his idea.

I went through the hole and dropped down onto the dusty floor of bare earth below, thinking how neat it was that this dirt was dry as could be, even when it was raining cats and dogs outside.

Except for the four square pillars that helped support the weight of the house, I had an unobstructed view. I could see the 18-inch high cement wall which surrounded the entire perimeter of the house, and which supported the entire structure. Outside the north wall, which ran just behind me, I could hear the sound of raindrops hitting the side of the house.

Across the bottom of the house strung east to west, were pieces of two by twelve inch lumber, running side by side about eighteen inches apart. The smell of the lumber, combined with the smell of the dark earth and the stale humid air, made for a unique aroma that I remember vividly today. It was rather pleasant.

Randy joined me below and we crawled around on all fours, exploring every inch of this forbidding place over the next couple of hours. By the time we resurfaced, we were filthy, sweaty, and absolutely thrilled with our find.

Randy occasionally went down after that, but nowhere as often as I did. I used to go under the house so often that I pilfered an old butter knife from my mom's silverware drawer. It was the knife that I kept hidden in my closet and used to pry open the trap door.

In the center of my hidden domain, directly under a floor grate in the hallway, was a pit about four feet square and three feet deep. It was in this pit that the floor furnace sat, before my father dismantled and removed it. He replaced it with a more efficient wall unit which was contained completely inside the house. So this pit was now vacant space.

I spent hundreds of hours sitting in that pit over the next couple of years, reading by candlelight or flashlight, or thinking, or daydreaming. Dirty as it was, it was my home away from home. I used to keep a stack of comic books there, and a water pistol to shoo away an occasional field mouse that invaded my world, and some of my old baseball cards. It was at this spot that I read The Adventures of Tom Sawyer for the first time, and 20,000 Leagues Under the Sea.

I learned from conversations with my friends that many of them, too, had their own secret places where they'd go to hide from the stresses of an adolescent world. Several of us even made a "blood pact" never to disclose one another's hide-outs. Those places were to remain ours and ours alone. To this day, none of my childhood friends knew where I went on the days when they came knocking on my door and nobody knew where I was.

I'd spend hours playing with beetles which lived in little burrows in the ground, or with the spiders that shared the space with me. My sisters were deathly afraid of spiders, but for some reason they didn't both me at all back then.

I don't recall whether I brought everything back up when I crawled out of that pit for the last time. Nor, for that matter, do I remember the last time I was there or the reason I stopped going there. I suppose I just outgrew that part of my childhood, in the same was I outgrew hot wheels tracks, skateboarding and playing marbles.

My dad still owns that house, although no one has lived in it for over 20 years. He uses it for storage now. I've been tempted for many years to go back to that house and crawl back into that pit. Some day I'll do it, and I'm looking forward to seeing what little treasures I'll find there.

Finding the Perfect Tree

When I was very young, the Christmas season was very special to me for a variety of reasons. First and foremost, of course, were the gifts. Any kid who tells anyone otherwise is just trying to score points.

But beyond the gifts, there were some wonderful and joyous things that we only got to do at that special time of year. Making popcorn garlands for our Christmas tree and hanging stockings up for Santa were a delight. So was our family tradition of leaving cookies and milk for Santa on Christmas Eve, along with a carrot for Rudolph.

But by far the greatest fun of the holiday season, at least at that stage in my life, was shopping for the family Christmas tree.

Artificial Christmas trees were around when I was a small boy. They just weren't used much. Today, some models do a pretty good job of imitating a real tree, but back then they looked absolutely ridiculous. No self-respecting family in my neighborhood would be caught dead with a tree that didn't grow from mother earth.

Consequently, there were several "Christmas tree lots" which sprang up around town in the weeks just prior to Christmas each year and closed down the day after Christmas. This was the only option for Lubbock residents who wanted a real tree, since the nearest pine or fir trees (or mountains, for that matter) were several hundred miles away. So every year, just before Christmas, we began our annual trek around town to find the perfect Christmas tree.

These journeys always began the same way. We'd drive by the first two or three lots without stopping. My father would roll down the window and hold his head out as he slowly drove by, blasting those of us in the back seat with frigid air.

"Nope," he'd say, "those are too skimpy."

After the first few lots failed to pass muster, Dad would lower his standards just a bit and cruise past the lots again.

Eventually a certain tree would catch his eye. "Hmmm," he'd finally say. "That one looks like it might be okay."

This was the signal which meant we were finally going to get out of the car.

Of course, the appearance of the tree was only one factor in determining which one we finally carried home. The other primary concern, since we were a family of limited means, was the price. More than once, I remember my dad asking the price of a particular tree, then turning without comment and merely walking away.

Eventually, we'd find a tree we liked that was reasonably priced. Before Dad made a final decision to purchase it, though, it had to pass two tests.

The first was the "needle test." He'd lift it up about a foot off the ground and slam the bottom of the trunk into the dirt. Then he'd move the tree to one side and see how many needles had dropped off. This was supposed to determine how dry the tree was, but I always suspected it was to give Dad a better bargaining position when it came time to negotiating a price.

The dryness test didn't always work, by the way. I remember one Christmas when we bought a tree so dry that the branches were completely barren by Christmas morning. The presents, on the other hand, were covered with a thick blanket of pine needles.

The second test was the "eyeball test." My mother would step back a few steps and closely examine the tree while my father slowly turned it. She was looking for bare spots that would make decorating the tree harder.

More often than not, we had to accept a few minor imperfections in order to get a good price for the tree. When positioning it in the living room, we sometimes had to turn it so that a bad spot faced the corner, or put extra decorations in certain places where the branches were thin.

Once purchased, Dad's ritual included asking the tree dealer for some rope to tie the tree to the car. Now, bear in mind that this was an annual ritual. Dad had rope in the garage from the year before. And from the year before that. But he never brought his own rope. I think he figured the section of rope a bonus for buying the tree. Perhaps it was his way of thinking he got just a little bit over on the tree salesman. Whatever his motives, Dad always had plenty of twelve-foot sections laying around the garage to be used for household projects.

Tying the tree down was a ritual in itself. Dad had this process down to a science.

First, he placed the tree on top of the car, with the top of the tree facing the rear. Then, opening both front doors, he ran the rope through the interior of the car and over the tree. He did this twice, and if the rope wasn't long enough, he asked for a second piece and tied them together.

Mom told us once about the first time Dad tied a tree down in this manner. He had rolled down the windows but closed the doors, and passed the rope through one window, through he car, and to my mom who was on the other side. Mom said it wasn't until they got the rope good and tight and tried to get into the car that they realized they had tied the doors shut.

Dad denied this story ever happened. I would have too.

My First Dance

I was asking some of my friends not long ago what types of things they remembered from their childhoods. I had expected the women to tell me about such things as their first love, their first kiss, and their first broken heart. And they did. But what surprised me, though, was that the men also remembered these things, and weren't afraid to admit it.

Of course, the guys also listed things the women didn't, like their first broken bone, the first time they went fishing or rode a motorcycle, and the first time they saw a dead body. The last one, I suppose, is an indication that a little boy's fascination for gruesome things never really goes away. Something else all of them remembered was the first prank they pulled on someone, or had pulled on them.

The point of all of this, finally, is that every one of my friends, men and woman alike, remembered one thing. Their first dance.

In my adolescence, I was head over heels in love with a good friend's sister. Her name was Kathy "with a 'K,'" she always said. She lived two blocks away and one block over, but she was in my dreams constantly for a long time.

A year younger than I, and all blonde hair and smiles, she was, as the old rhyme goes, "sugar and spice and everything nice."

One sunny day in my twelfth year, Kathy and I found ourselves at a birthday party at Ronnie Roscoe's house. Ronnie lived about half a block down from me, on the same side of the street, and was the friend I hung out with every time I got into trouble and had my street-crossing rights taken away for a couple of days.

It hadn't taken me long to accept the invitation to Ronnie's party. It was at his house, at his party the year prior, that I got to kiss Kathy for the first (and only) time, during an impromptu game of "spin the bottle."

The second party had more or less the same crowd, which is to say that all the kids on the block were invited, and most of them came. The activities were also more or less unchanged from the previous year, with the boys playing a game of baseball in the back yard and the girls playing with Barbie dolls in the house.

One additional treat were the live catfish that Ronnie's dad brought home from a fishing trip that morning. They were swimming around in three large wash tubs, barely still alive, and were fascinating for all of the boys at the party. Even more fascinating was being able to help Ronnie's dad cut off their heads and clean the fish for the Roscoe's dinner that evening.

By the time we went inside the house for cake and ice cream, all the boys smelled like sweat and fish. It didn't bother us. But it sure generated a lot of complaints from the girls, and Ronnie's mom let her husband know in no uncertain terms that she was not pleased.

"Aw, they're boys," he protested. "They like stuff like that."

He was in the dog house for the rest of the afternoon. He cut himself a big chunk of cake, took some vanilla ice cream from the bucket he'd churned for the occasion, and punched Ronnie on the arm.

"Happy birthday, Bucko," he said. Then he leaned close to Ronnie's face, winked, and said "Don't ever get married."

Then he went and sat on his easy chair, turned on his news, and sulked.

After the birthday song was sung, the wishes made and the cake eaten, the presents were opened and the mess cleaned up, the "official" festivities were winding to a close. A couple of the guests left, and the remaining girls made an announcement.

As they had the year before, the girls had schemed among themselves while the guys were outside playing ball. This year, instead of repeating the previous party's game of "spin the bottle," they decided to have a dance.

I'd have rather spun the bottle and kissed Kathy a second time, but, yeah, okay, a dance would work. At least I'd get to hold her hand and put my arm around her.

All of the other boys groaned at the idea. Mrs. Roscoe breathed an audible sigh of relief. She seemed to accept this as a much better alternative than the previous year's after party activities.

Danny, Kathy's little brother, immediately said "no way!" and bolted for the back door. His older brother Johnny, on the other hand, agreed to hang around and dance "just one time."

This was a marked change from the previous year's party, when the bottle was first brought out and he beat little Danny to the back door.

I think that Johnny was smitten with Ronnie's cousin, a little red-haired girl with blue eyes and braces.

One of the girls ran home for some records, and twenty minutes later we were trying to find Ronnie's mom's 45 RPM adapter so we could play some music.

You youngsters won't remember, but back then single records had a large hole in the middle of them. Since record players were made primarily for 33 RPM albums, an adapter was required to place the smaller singles onto the record player's spindle. If that makes no sense to you, then you're obviously still wet behind the ears.

After considerable searching, Mrs. Roscoe found the adapter and Kathy and I found ourselves very awkwardly dancing to the songs of the Jackson 5 and the Osmonds. Hey, don't laugh. It was a long time ago, and I didn't get to pick the music.

I remember thinking, though, how cool we were, dancing smoothly around to the strains of "ABC" and "Puppy Love." In retrospect, I probably looked more like a lumberjack standing on a log in the middle of a raging river, trying desperately to keep his balance and stay upright.

No matter. It was my first dance, and it happened to be with a girl I was very fond of, and it'll always occupy a special place in my memory. To this day, whenever I happen to hear "Puppy Love" or "ABC" on a golden oldie station, my mind will go back instantly in time to that small frame house on 32nd Street where I tried so hard to sweep a young girl off of her feet. I can still smell the catfish too…

A few months later I moved to San Antonio for a spell, and by the time I moved back to Lubbock three years later, Kathy, Danny and Johnny had moved away. None of my friends could remember where they moved to, and that stung for a bit. At least until the next cute girl caught my eye.

But there can only be one first broken bone, or dead body, or whatever, and the same holds true for my very first dance. In the deep recesses of my mind, "Puppy Love" will play until I draw my last breath.

Wherever you are, Kathy, thanks for the dance.

Painted Grass

When my good friend Dennis Bryant told me they painted the grass green at the First Federal savings and Loan building, I thought he was pulling my leg. It was the middle of December, Christmas lights were strung on all the houses in our neighborhood, and there wasn't a blade of green grass anywhere for 500 miles. In fact, a week before we'd had a couple of inches of snow on the ground. The idea of green grass this time of year, painted or not, was ludicrous. Besides, why would anyone paint grass? I was just a dumb kid, and even I knew that was a stupid idea.

"It's true! Come and see for yourself!" Dennis pleaded, obviously irked that I questioned his word.

Dennis wheeled his bicycle around and Mark and I climbed on our Schwinns. Mark's was cooler than mine because he had the banana seat and a sissy bar with an Esso tiger tail flying from the top. Some kids are luckier than others.

Or maybe not. Mark got about twenty feet and ground to a stop. He looked at his rear tire and saw that it was flat as a pancake. He must have picked up a sticker.

Now, back then we all carried dog bone wrenches and patch kits on out bikes. It was the "cool" accessory of the moment. He could have changed the tire in no time at all, but he said his hands were numb from the cold.

So we parked our bikes and walked the two blocks to First Federal.

On the way Mark told Dennis and I that his dad was giving him grief about riding his bike in the wintertime anyway. He'd seen a kid riding his bike and sliding on an ice patch into an oncoming car, and told Mark he didn't want the same thing to happen to his only son.

The three of us agreed that Mark's dad must never have been a kid himself. If he had been, he'd have known that riding a bike on icy streets and sidewalks was much more fun than riding it in dry sunny weather. That's because the daredevil in every boy loves to slip and slide and wipe out occasionally. If these mishaps produce an occasional bruise or broken bone, that's okay. It's just the price boys pay for this simple pleasure.

Besides, bruises and broken bones are badges of honor for adolescent boys.

Anyway, I remember the bitter wind blowing that morning that froze my ears until they went numb. My dad's haircut of choice was a burr, which these days is called a buzz cut, and basically means that every bit of hair on your head comes off, and there isn't any left to keep your head warm. Or to cover your ears.

Unfortunately for me, dad loved his hairstyle so much that he always instructed our barber to give me the same one. Thanks, Dad.

Anyway, so there we were, frozen ears and all, half a block from First Federal Savings and Loan when we caught sight of the green grass and stopped dead in our tracks. Then we burst out laughing.

Dennis' credibility was restored. It turned out that the savings and loan branch had indeed painted their grass a bright springtime green. It looked absolutely outrageous.

As I've said many times in the past, young boys don't let things like common sense and logic get in the way of their wishes. Although deep down inside we probably all knew better, we walked on the grass to see if painting it somehow made it soft and plush.

It crunched beneath our feet.

Then Dennis had an idea: "It looks like a football field. Let's play ball!"

It sounded like a good idea, since there wasn't anything else to do this chilly Sunday afternoon. First Federal was closed, so they shouldn't mind too much. My ears were already numb from the cold, so I had nothing to lose by staying out in the weather. And since Mark's house was closest, and because he had the best football, he volunteered to run home and get the ball.

Dennis and I crossed the street to the Preston's Milk Store while Mark was gone. We pooled our change and split a cup of hot chocolate and a package of Now and Laters.

Mark came trotting back about fifteen minutes later. (In the 1960s, nobody jogged. They trotted. For some reason, this term faded into obscurity, like many other terms of the period, such as groovy, neat-o and "peace, man")

Phil Brasher's family wagon drove by on their way home from church, and he joined us a few minutes later. He said it looked like more fun than anything else going on at his house.

As usual, our football game started out friendly and grew more and more rowdy as we went on. We officially played "two below," which meant a ball carrier was considered tackled when a defender touched him with two hands anywhere below the waist. However, playing tackle was just more fun, so normally we were playing all-out tackle, bordering on brawling, by the time we finished each game.

After half an hour, we began to notice that the grass where we'd been playing was no longer green. In fact, there was no longer any grass there. Everywhere someone had fallen, or been tackled, there was a brown spot where the bare dirt showed through.

Worse, we were covered with green dye from head to toe. Our jeans, jackets, and most of the exposed parts of our bodies were bright green. We looked like martians, only without the big heads.

All we could do was look at each other and laugh uproariously. We looked ridiculous.

When it finally dawned on us that we had ruined First Federal's newly painted lawn, we decided it was a good time to go find something else to do. We high-tailed it back home and spent a good part of the evening scrubbing our hands and faces with Lava soap, trying to restore their natural color.

I remember going to school the next day and trying to hide my hands, because they still had a very distinctive green tint to them.

Times have certainly changed. I was talking to Mark not long ago and he mentioned this adventure. He commented that if this same thing were to happen today to a group of boys from the current generation, their moms probably would have sued First Federal for the damage done to the boys' clothes, skin and psyches.

Back then things were different. Nobody sued anybody. We did go by First Federal a couple of days later and apologized for ruining their paint job. As I recall, they took it pretty well. Probably wrote it off as a business expense. But they never painted their grass again, and I wondered if they thought it looked as ridiculous as we did. Or maybe they thought we'd just destroy it again. It would have been safe from us, though. We'd learned our lesson.

Here's a free tip: If you're ever tempted to paint your grass in the dead of winter, don't waste the time and energy. You won't fool anybody. Even the dumbest of dumb kids will not believe it's the grass's natural color that time of year. And, you'll stand a good chance that a handful of young boys will come along and mess it up for you.

Take it from me.

Clark's Department Store

These days, I can't seem to return to my hometown without taking a slow drive through the old neighborhood where I grew up so many years ago. I frequently stop and marvel at the changes, noticing how a particular house has been torn down since the last time I was there, or an old gas station has been turned into a muffler shop, or an aging building now has a condemned sign hanging on its door.

One old building that always catches my eye is the old Clark's Department Store on Avenue Q. Now a car dealer, this huge building was built in the 1950s, and for many years housed a rather large department store. That's what they used to call discount stores before Wal-Mart and K-Mart came along.

Clark's was, in a way, a forerunner to Wal-Mart. It was a huge operation that sold a little bit of everything, with a long bank of checkout counters in the front of the store and a bevy of young employees saying "may I help you?" by rote to every living, breathing being in sight.

For a long time I refused to walk into that car dealer's showroom. I reasoned that it was much better to preserve the memory of how Clark's used to be in my feeble little mind, than to see the inside of the building as it is today.

The last time I was in Lubbock, I finally broke down. I parked my car and walked into the dealership, under the guise of shopping for a new vehicle. I was really there to see how the interior of the building had changed, secretly hoping that it was exactly the way it was the last time I was in the building in 1968.

I was pleasantly surprised at how my memories came flooding back to me. Although the building had undergone extensive renovation after the store closed down all those years ago, I found myself pacing on the same stretch of floor that I had played on as a young boy. Everywhere I stood or looked took on an otherworldly vision of what used to be there.

I looked at the north wall, near the front of the showroom, and remembered the soda machine that once stood there. It was of a type seldom seen today, except perhaps in the break rooms of older office buildings in large cities. After dropping in a few coins, the purchaser selected a drink, pushed a little white button, and watched as a small paper cup dropped from a hidden chute onto a small slotted platform. Directly over the platform were several spigots which pumped carbonated water and flavored syrup into the cup, along with crushed ice. The concoction mixed, as if by magic, to create the requested flavor of soda. The result was not unlike a typical beverage bar product in any fast food restaurant in America today. Only this machine did everything for you, and to a young boy it was a thing of wonder. I still vividly remember peering up into the mysterious chute and trying to figure out how this magical marvel worked.

Leaning against the side of this machine, four decades ago, was a mop handle, attached to an old cloth mop, which was as much a permanent fixture as the machine itself.

Because so many of Clark's patrons had a habit of spilling a portion of their drinks as they lifted them from the machine, store employees kept the mop nearby, and mopped up the area in front of the machine several times a day. I remember how the checkerboard tiles on the floor were discolored and coming up on the edges from the constant remopping.

The discolored tiles, of course, are gone forever, except in the deep recesses of my memory.

As I walked about the showroom, occasionally shooing away a pesky young salesman who wanted to explain the virtues of the various automobiles, I was surprised at the number of memories this old building brought back. I very clearly remembered running through the store every time we came, trying to beat my brother and sisters to the toy department. Right there, next to that column in the southern part of the building, were the three aisles that stocked a wide range of toys so many years ago.

Since my family lived on a tight budget, there were many things we saw, in magazines or on television, that we simply could not afford to buy. A visit to Clark's was sometimes our only opportunity to play with some of the latest and greatest toys on the market.

Clark's employees always opened up many of the new toys and left them on the floor in the toy section for kids to play with while their parents shopped. This might have been a marketing ploy, to encourage the kids to fall in love with the toys and then twist their parents' arms to buy them. I prefer to think of it, though, as a courtesy to the parents, to get the kids out of their hair while the parents shopped. Perhaps too, it was just a nice gesture for the kids themselves. In any event, I never would have been able to play with "Rock 'em, Sock 'em Robots," or "G.I. Joe with Kung-Fu Grip" if that hadn't been the store policy at Clark's.

As I wandered through the car dealer's showroom, other things came back to me. Right there, along the wall leading to the restrooms, was where my little brother Randy threw up while Christmas shopping in 1966. A little farther back was where the jewelry counter stood, when I came on my bike with a pocketful of change to buy my mother some cheap earrings for her birthday. Over there was the shoe department, where we used to buy my canvas Keds, black with three white racing stripes.

Outside the store, under a covered pavilion, had been a row of coin-operated amusement rides. Forget the race car or the fire truck. Those were for the little kids. I preferred the helicopter, because it was much cooler. For my nickel, I got a ride that rocked back and forth and made helicopter sounds. It even had a propeller on top that slowly rotated when the ride was in motion.

The brash young salesman finally gave up on me. He probably thought I was a nut, since I spent more time looking at the building's walls and floors than at his shiny new cars. Of course, he had no way of knowing about the friendly ghosts I had seen walking around that building, or the memories that had come rushing back to me while I was there. He hadn't even been born yet when Clark's closed its doors for the last time.

Now I regret waiting so many years before going back into that building. It was a very pleasant experience, and I'll visit there again sometime. Wilder once said you can never go home again. He was wrong. Home is still there, in our memories. We just need to encourage it to come out and play sometimes.

Taco

Taco certainly wasn't much to look at. A mangy, flea-bitten mixed breed with crossed eyes and lop-ears, calling him a "mutt" was the kindest way to describe him.

Not that Taco wasn't likeable. As ugly as he was, the kids in my neighborhood on Bane Street in San Antonio thought the world of him. He was everything a boy wanted in a dog. He was friendly, loyal, and intelligent enough to do a limited number of tricks. We liked Taco just fine. It was just too bad he didn't belong to any of us.

Taco stood about a foot high at the shoulders, his dirty and matted fur about the same rich yellow color as the corn tortillas we used for taco shells. We surmised that was the reason for his name, although we never knew for sure. There was a tuft of hair on the middle of his back that was perfectly straight, although the rest of his hair was as curly as Shirley Temple's. Kiko's dad said that was a sign of inbreeding, and warned us that such dogs were sometimes vicious. But he didn't really know Taco like we did.

The only vicious tendencies we ever saw was the treatment of Taco by his owner, Mr. Ramos. None of us had the nerve to talk to Mr. Ramos, a monster of a man who lived at the end of our street. As ugly as Taco was, his owner was ten times worse. Perhaps it was because of his appearance that we were afraid of him. That, plus we saw the way he treated Taco, and we suspected we'd fare no better. We were nine and ten years old at the time, and saw that even the adults of the neighborhood steered clear of Mr. Ramos. So we did the same.

Taco ran free most of the time, and followed us everywhere. When we went to the quarry that summer to play or to fish, he quietly followed a few paces behind. When we'd stop to rest, he'd find the sparse shade of a nearby mesquite tree and lay beneath it, watching and waiting for us to continue on our way. Then he'd get up to follow, his tongue hanging limply from his mouth and flies buzzing around his face.

The first time we picked up a stick in Taco's presence it was obvious that he was beaten on a regular basis. We wanted to see if he would play fetch, but at the first sign of the stick he yelped and ran in the other direction. It took considerable prodding to convince him that we meant no harm. Once we gained his trust, he took to fetching in no time at all. I think he especially enjoyed the praise and the pat on the head he got each time he returned the stick to us.

At the quarry, we learned that Taco was an excellent swimmer. He'd jump into the small playa lake, and we'd run around to the other side and call his name. He'd swim toward us, and we'd wait until he got almost to the shore, before we'd run to the other side of the lake and repeat the process. Doggedly, (no pun intended) he'd turn around, reverse his course, and begin paddling toward us again. He'd eventually wear us out, because we'd get tired of running before he'd get tired of swimming. When he was finally able to tromp out of the water, knowing that he'd won the game, he'd romp over to where we were and shake water all over us. That, it seemed, was his reward for winning. But we didn't mind. More often than not, we'd wrestle with him until all four of us were soaked and smelling like wet dogs.

We eventually taught Taco to sit, roll over, and play dead. We seemed to make a good team, this canine misfit and us, for at that awkward time in our lives we all felt sometimes that no one understood or wanted us. The difference was that my friends and I all had comfortable beds to sleep in at night. Taco had to go home each night to the brutal treatment of Mr. Ramos.

Each evening about sundown, Mr. Ramos would stand by his back door and yell Taco's name. This sent chills up our spines, for we all knew what was to follow. After a few minutes we'd hear his curses and the sounds of him whipping and kicking this poor creature. Then we'd hear Taco's subdued yelps and whimpers, as he nursed his wounds long into the night.

His owner seemed most upset that Taco wandered off each day, yet he certainly offered him no good reason to stay. There were no fences or pens to keep Taco at home, and this miserable man seemed not to care that dogs like to explore. They also like to be treated with kindness, which might be why Taco seemed to find my friends and I whenever we went out to play.

One day Tony Montoya announced to us that his family was moving to the other side of the city. As sad as we were to see our good friend go, we saw this as a golden opportunity to help another friend, our lop-eared buddy, to get away from Mr. Ramos for good.

The day after Tony's family moved away, he and his dad returned and pulled into Kiko's driveway. Tony had confided to his dad that we needed his help in "dog napping" Taco and providing him with a better home. It turned out that most of the adults in the neighborhood were also aware of Taco's misfortune, and he readily agreed to the plan.

When Tony opened up the back door of his dad's car and tried to coax Taco in, Taco looked confused and refused to budge. He turned and looked at us, then at Tony, then at the dog biscuit that Tony's dad had placed on the back seat to lure him in. It wasn't until Tony himself crawled into the back seat that Taco followed.

That night Mr. Ramos called Taco's name many times over the course of a couple of hours, but of course the dog never responded. By that time, he was the only one in the neighborhood who didn't know that Taco now had a better home, on the other side of San Antonio, and a new family that would treat him well.

A few days later Kiko gathered several pieces of Taco's waste from the yard and moistened them, then put them in a paper bag. Late that night he put the bag on Mr. Ramos' porch, lit it on fire, and rang the doorbell. We watched from a distance as Mr. Ramos stamped out the flames in his bedroom slippers, smearing the waste all over himself and his porch. Over the next few weeks, we frequently took turns sneaking over to Mr. Ramos' house at all hours of the night and ringing his doorbell. More than just typical childish pranks, our actions felt like vindication for our friend Taco and all that he had endured.

I never saw Tony or Taco again. But I know that Taco lived out the remainder of his years in a good home, and was never again beaten merely for being himself.

The Little Green Store

If you drive into my hometown of Lubbock, Texas today and drive to the intersection of 35th and Avenue W, you'll find a little rock-faced structure in front of a massive water tower.

Today, this tiny building houses an equally small marketing business, and the people working there have no clue of the building's past. They also have no idea that the building holds a special place in my heart, as well as the hearts of hundreds of other children of my generation, who were lucky enough to grow up in that great neighborhood.

Once upon a time, this structure housed a small grocery store, which was visited by dozens of kids daily on their way to and from school, or on their lunch breaks. When I was a kid, it was covered not with rock, but with pale green asbestos shingles. Knowing that fact, it's easier to understand why this building was known in the 1960s to the entire neighborhood as "the little green store."

I'm sure that this mom and pop store had a proper name, although I don't have a clue what it was. I vaguely remember an old sign on the face of the building that said "Market," but I can't for the life of me remember the name that preceded it. No one else I've ever talked to can remember it either. They can all remember its other, informal name though. The little green store was so much a part of our lives back then that even today it elicits warm smiles when I talk about it with people that were there.

Even in the 1960s, this tiny frame building seemed ancient. Walking in, the grocer's bell at the top of the door would signal our presence and alert the proprietors that they had a customer.

The couple who ran the place were probably in their mid-60s, but appeared much older. I give them the benefit of a few years because I know that to kids, old people always appear to be older than they really are.

In any event, they both had the grizzled look that a hard life instills on someone, and the man walked slightly stooped. The woman moved quite slowly, and gave the impression that every movement caused her pain.

Both seemed friendly enough, though, and sometimes talked of their grandchildren. They never seemed to grow impatient when it took us forever to select what we wanted, and they always smiled and thanked us for our meager purchases. The woman had a habit of asking how we were doing in school, or whether we were working hard and making good grades. It wasn't the idle chatter you get from a clerk at a modern day 7-11. It was the kindly and genuine voice of a grandmother.

For our pennies and nickels, we had a variety of candies to choose from. My sister would always buy something called a "Cherry Mash," which was a chunk of cherry-flavored confection covered with chocolate and crushed peanuts. They weren't bad, but they couldn't beat the penny licorice that came out of a jar, one strand at a time. Each piece was about a yard long, as think as a piece of spaghetti, and despite its name, actually cost three cents. A perfect snack for a small boy of limited means.

Another favorite, which my good friend Wesley loved, was a long plastic straw-like tube filled with grape-flavored sugar. I can't remember what this candy was called, but I recall it turning Wesley's tongue, and often half his face, a hideous purple color. His facial discoloration often made "grape boy" the butt of jokes at school.

I remember a surprising number of customers who utilized this little market for an odd food item or two. It was more or less the forerunner of the modern convenience store, I suppose, in that it stocked only the bare essentials, and did most of its business in milk, bread, cigarettes and snacks.

There was a Preston's Milk Store only a block away that never seemed to do as much business as the little green store. Although the Preston's had a larger inventory with a lot better selection, and even had an Icee machine, they charged considerably more for their wares. And they didn't have a sweet set of grandparental-types working for them.

Even kids who weren't wise to the ways of the world knew how to comparison shop, and if we could buy a little more for the same meager change by walking a block, we'd do it. That's why the little green store got our business whenever they were open.

The other reason we enjoyed going there, I suppose, was the atmosphere. I haven't been in a chain convenience store yet which is half as friendly as an old "mom and pop" store.

We lose something as a culture every time one of these small grocery stores closes down. In these days, where it seems everything is owned by big corporations and is sanitized, pre-packaged and franchised, we've forgotten that this country was built by the small entrepreneur. It's a real shame that most of them have gone away.

I haven't got a clue when the little green store went out of business. I suspect that in the end Preston's won out and took away so much of their business that it was no longer profitable for them. Or maybe they just got too old to run the store, and retired of their own free will. In either case, I really miss the option of stopping in for a soda whenever I'm in my old neighborhood.

I asked the workers at the marketing agency if they had soda for sale and they thought I was crazy. Some people just have no sense of humor at all.

Made in the USA
Lexington, KY
16 November 2012